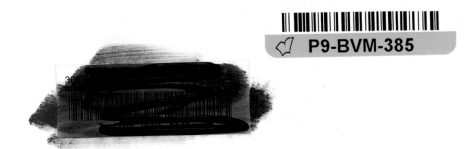

P9-BVM-385

The Meaning of Children

Other Titles in This Series

Also of Interest

Westview Special Studies in Contemporary Social Issues

The Meaning of Children: Attitudes and Opinions of a Selected Group of U.S. University Graduates

Eulah Croson Laucks

As more individuals delay having children or opt for childlessness, the question arises: What value do people place on children in contemporary U.S. society? Dr. Laucks studies this question through a survey designed to elicit attitudes regarding the purpose and desirability of raising children in the context of a depersonalized, fragmented, and alienating society.

The survey—of a large group of university graduates—points to marked discrepancies between individual attitudes favoring procreation and parenthood and individual actions that contradict traditional notions. Purported aspirations and goals still include the hope of raising happy, healthy children. Yet, while individually valuing children and family, Americans widely approve of and use contraceptives and other birth control methods, endorse easy dissolution of marriage, and approve of relationships that exclude children. The author examines these diverging attitudes in relation to contemporary and historical sentiments toward the family.

Extensive tables display the detailed results of Dr. Laucks's survey, giving demographic information on the respondents, along with their attitudes toward sexual practices, parenthood, child rearing, and the family.

Dr. Laucks is president of Laucks Foundation, Inc., a member of the board of directors of Channel City Women's Forum, and a member of the steering committee of the Robert M. Hutchins Center for the Study of Democratic Institutions at the University of California, Santa Barbara.

The Meaning of Children

Attitudes and Opinions of a Selected Group of U.S. University Graduates

Eulah Croson Laucks

Westview Press / Boulder, Colorado

Westview Special Studies in Contemporary Social Issues

Published in 1981 in the United States of America by
Westview Press, Inc.
5500 Central Avenue
Boulder, Colorado 80301
Frederick A. Praeger, Publisher

Library of Congress Cataloging in Publication Data
Laucks, Eulah.
The meaning of children.
(Westview special studies in contemporary social issues)
Bibliography: p.
1. Children—Public opinion. 2. Public opinion—United States. I. Title.
HQ792.U5L38   305.2'3'0973   80-12111
ISBN 0-89158-881-7

Printed and bound in the United States of America

For
Irving, Mary, and Lorenzo

Contents

Figures and Tables

Acknowledgments

I am indebted to Professors Walter H. Capps, Charles B. Spaulding, and W. Elliot Brownlee of the University of California, Santa Barbara, without whose counsel and encouragement this work would never have come into being.

Eulah Croson Laucks

The Meaning of Children

1
Introduction

In a study attempting to determine what meaning *children* may have for a given people or society, some prior questions should be asked that have to do with how the *family* as a whole is regarded by such people or society. Hence, in this study of the meaning of children in the contemporary United States, the following questions have been posed for prior consideration: Is the *family* valuable today for individual Americans? Is some recognizably homogeneous form of family indispensable to the well-being of U.S. society?

When I first began research on the family, I took as given the premise that the family is the rock upon which society stands, and that, to a large degree, the nature of the family determines the kind of society that will emerge in a given place. It followed, I thought, that if society were to be changed for the better, efforts at improvement would have to begin with the family.

After a decade of study, however, I have come to think that, paradoxically, although the family may be a necessary foundation stone upon which society rests, it is society that determines what the family will be, and not the other way around. Whatever family form (or forms) a given society requires for its own impetus and prolongation is likely to be the kind (or kinds) of family that will, perforce, develop. Hence, if the family is to be improved or changed, efforts in that direction will have to be aimed first — or at least simultaneously — at society. That means at the whole web of politico-economic institutions and leadership.

I think of the family as being what we *are* as a nation at any given point, and of society as being how we *act*. There seems to be a discrepancy, or lag, between what individuals are in a society and what they are doing as a collectivity. Today, this lag may be so great and our life pace so rapid that we may not even be able to comprehend the results of our actions, much less discriminate what we are letting form our character as a nation. It is no wonder, then, that as individual human beings and as members of families many Americans are confused, adrift, and alienated from what seems to be the mainstream of our society.

Actually, the statement that the family may be at least one necessary foundation stone of society may not be true today. When societies are more or less homogeneous in character, the family may be said to be bedrock for human community. In a time, however, when society is fragmented and depersonalized, as it is in our country today, familism, at least in recognizable traditional form, may no longer function as foundation for community action. Hence, the pivotal question now may *not* be, do we as individuals *want* the family? (although I think that in any age that is the valid question), but rather, does society *need* the family as we have known it?

Demographically, contemporary society does not need the family. Widely authenticated statistics confirm that the world soon will be approaching a state of overpopulation. Our planet does not need more people for optimal use and husbandry of available resources. Demographically for the future that is widely predicted, the technotronic world (impelled by technology and electronic media) might get along very well with a few strategically placed human breeding installations.

With respect to health, education, and welfare, formerly thought to be the responsibility of the family, our country's vast public welfare apparatus is potentially capable of taking care of any foreseeable requirements. Schools in our country have taken over a great many other parental duties. And to further reduce traditional family functions, foster homes, babysitters, and day-care centers could be expanded to suit requirements. And economically, society no longer needs the great labor force concentrations that the traditional family helped stabilize and promote.

The self-serving needs of private citizens — ego reinforcement and name and gene survival — have perhaps no urgent societal functions now. The bio-programmed society that seems possible in the future could not only do without personalized needs — it would doubtless find them a hindrance.

Is the family necessary today for the support of female citizens? Women as individuals, and collectively in the women's liberation movement, are demonstrating that women can earn their own livelihoods and not necessarily be dependent on men for economic sustenance. Without social stigma, men now can avoid taking financial responsibility for "helpmates" by hiring cooks and maids to maintain their households. Sex requirements for both men and women doubtless could be bureaucratized or otherwise programmed.

Richard Boeth, general editor of *Newsweek*, observed a few years ago, "For the first time in recorded history, society has no legitimate reason to prevent men and women from going and coming, loving or not loving, as they please."[1] He further implied that the commitment to loving faithfulness in family life has never been more than a romanticized compromise with the needs of society. This, of course, is debatable; however, it might well be asked whether the societal horse that seems to be running away with us should not be reined in. Is the family an institution for the nurture and betterment of people, or is it simply a useful adjunct of our public actions, now gone wild? If it is true that society *does* need the family, should we not, then, consider what future forms, or transitional forms, are likely to emerge, and try, individually and as a national community, to exert some reasoned guidance for their development?

Historians disagree as to the origin of the traditional nuclear family as we know it in this country, composed only of parents and their children. Most researchers acknowledge that it probably came into being about 200 years ago. Before that, and back to the Middle Ages in Europe, the configurations of households did not emphasize individual consanguineous nuclei. There were polyglot combinations of near and far relatives, indentured servants, and indentured children from other families, all more or less communally concentrated for economic purposes. Children, at what was called the "age of reason" (about seven), were to all intents and purposes adult. To the extent of their capacities, they took part in the celebration of all communal games and festivities, as well as work, as if they were adults. There was no generation gap of interests, and there was no emphasis on privacy and recognition of individual family groupings.

As the Industrial Revolution developed, all this changed. Children became more important as children, and their activities and those of their parents began to diverge. What schooling experience there was, was taken out of the home and its span lengthened. Families began to grow self-centered. Increasingly, parents oriented children toward careers of parental choice. Individual private property became important. As capitalistic industry grew, the nuclear family became a device for expanding and perpetuating private fortunes. People of lesser means became infected with the Horatio Alger syndrome, and the "American dream" was born. Much later, especially with the advent and widespread distribution of motion pictures, the myth of the "happy American family" became accepted as a realizable goal for everybody. Most nations rear children to be happy in spite of their environment. Americans have been reared to "live happily ever after" and must learn to face disillusionment.

During the Victorian era, when children were "seen and not heard," the family solidified into strict separation of parents and children. Offspring were usually delegated to nannies and governesses, or, in the case of the impoverished, largely left to fend for themselves. The prevalent

Victorian consensus—at least among the upper classes who set styles and customs—was that what was least annoying to parents was best for children.

As the teachings of people like Sigmund Freud ("the child is father to the neurotic") gradually became assimilated into social custom, child nurture changed and rigid notions concerning inflexible toilet training of infants, and prohibitions against thumb sucking and masturbation were discarded in favor of "ego strengthening." Thus, not only children but also parents grew neurotic. People ill-equipped for the task became psychiatrists to their children. The era of the guilt-ridden, anxious, ineffectual parent was upon the country, and the seeds of disintegration were sown in the traditional family structure. Parents faced the dilemma of the tension between doing what they felt was good for the development of the child and what they (the parents) could stand by way of undisciplined noise, sloppiness, destructiveness, and so on.

The "togetherness" of the '50s then gave rise to the confusion of the '60s when frustration followed disillusionment, as ever-expanding technological forces closed in on the family, along with war, riots, student revolts, and assassinations.

Today—with the assertiveness of women, rights for homosexuals, the birth control pill, permissive attitudes toward love in and out of marriage; with the rise in use of paid babysitters and day-care centers; with the ease and prevalence of divorce and the growing rate of single-parent families—it can be said surely that the traditional nuclear family, as a homogeneity in this country, stands in disarray if not in a fairly advanced state of disintegration. At best these days, the family manages to hold together as a unified and functioning entity until the children are grown. The sad truth is that too many American families have become, in effect, places for individual members to hang their hats while "doing their own thing" or waiting for a "better pad to hop to."

It was said of the Loud family, who appeared in the television documentary "American Family" a few years ago, that they were not a *typical* American family. As portrayed, neither were they unique. The tremendous impression the series made on the U.S. public at the time was sufficient indication that a chord of recognition was struck in the hearts of many people. In an article in the *New York Times* at the time of the broadcasts, John O'Connor observed that the documentary posed serious questions about values, relationships, and institutions; about a constantly consuming society and our accelerating treadmills to meaningless status; and about avoiding problems at any cost.[2]

About the "everything-is-okay" syndrome depicted, Craig Gilbert, the producer of the series, commented that the Louds did not communicate about the "bad stuff." He said that is the way we are as a country and that is what the series was about — the fact that we Americans can never admit that we have made a mistake. The habit of pretending there are no problems — that everything, in Mrs. Loud's words, is "keen," is one of the phenomena we might point to as typical of *the* American family. Americans do have a tendency to imagine that their lives are actually very like the models put before them by Hollywood and television. Only lately have we begun questioning the meaning of some of our attitudes toward this playacting way of life.

An enumeration of significant social changes over the past quarter century that have impinged on family structure and function would include the following:

1. Governmental and other bureaucracies have expanded to the point of handling almost everything for the individual citizen. The individual is close to feeling that he has become little more than a number in society.

2. Society generally has become depersonalized. With the spread of instant communications, we have lost our sense of privacy. Everything in the world happens right in our living rooms. Also, instant awareness of remote real happenings has given rise to casual acceptance of them as if they are entertainment rather than depictions of reality. On the screen we watch stark actuality of brutality and violent death while reaching with scarce interruption for our favorite snack food.

3. Schools have assumed the function of performing many parental tasks including health care.

4. Wide habituation to consumer credit has brought with it conditioning to instant gratification, which has led to the withering of capacities for self-discipline and sacrifice. This, in turn, has reinforced toleration of the kind of "throwaway" society we now have. Likewise, pride in doing a good job has eroded.

5. We have become a nomadic society. One writer refers to our American way of life as "the mobile acquisitive society." Twenty percent of Americans have moved annually for the past twenty years. The automobile and the airplane have rendered the moving of households, as well as holiday travel, quick, available, and easy. Half the U.S. population does not live in its natal state. Neighborhoods and communities have ceased to be very important as hubs for family activities.

6. There has been homogenization of styles and expectations, due mainly to exposure to television, motion pictures, and travel. Mention should be made of what television commercial advertising has done to hammer us all into homogenized consumers.

7. There has been a constant and widespread scattering of interests and activities of family members. We have been segregated ever more

sharply into age groups. Generation gaps have opened at five-year intervals.

8. As a result of activities of the women's liberation movement, equal opportunity legislation, and the fact that over 40 percent of mothers are working outside the home, we have moved into a period when babysitting and child-care centers have become as indispensable as laundry service and milk delivery.

9. Divorce has been made quick and fairly painless, and no longer carries the deterring stigma of social censure. There are now at least 16 million divorced people in the United States. Extralegal cohabitation and birth control have become generally accepted phenomena. Abortion has been legalized by the Supreme Court and the right to use it at will has become widely and openly defended.

10. First marriages have dropped sharply since the advent of the birth control pill, and divorced people are not remarrying at as high a rate as formerly. Divorced status is a permanent and accepted phenomenon in the culture. Men have come to taking custody of their children in divorce situations. Women are less stigmatized now for giving up their children. In some cases, they are even refusing to assume the single responsibility of raising their children. In the last few years, the number of children living with divorced fathers has risen appreciably. One rather startling development in recent years has been that sometimes *neither* parent wants custody of children. Chief Judge John R. Evans of the Denver Juvenile Court observed that throughout the country "we are having a wholesale abdication of parental responsibility."[3]

11. A writer for *Newsweek* magazine commented not long ago that what we think of as the virtues that draw us to marriage—the yearning for routine, for permanence and security—are in this restless, volatile time the very things that drive us to the divorce courts.[4] Edward Grossman, writing about the troubled state of the contemporary American family, said that some anthropologists and psychiatrists, "with considerable powers to shape the *Zeitgeist,* have constructed systems in which the family replaces money as the root of all evil."[5] Margaret Mead repeatedly observed that the nuclear form of the family is the worst ever devised.

The paradox is that in spite of all adverse vicissitudes, the American dream of a traditional family is very much alive today. Deeply, indelibly, as a people, Americans still think in terms of a stable, recognizable familial commitment. It seems that this, doggedly, is what ordinary Americans are and want. And from this, advocates of familism may take hope. Yet, family stability and commitment in this nation are far from generally realized. A great many Americans act—or are impelled by the pace and impingement of the technological juggernaut that encompasses them — as if traditional family values no longer are of much worth in contemporary U.S. society. The discrepancy between familial notions and societal actions — between what people are and desire and how they act in community — remains wide and may be widening. The questions that attempt to probe the meaning of children in the contemporary United States have been framed in this context.

The next chapter presents some notes on historical attitudes toward children followed by a chapter on contemporary trends affecting the meaning of children. Chapters 4 and 5 contain a description and explanation of a survey carried out to elicit contemporary attitudes and opinions with respect to children. The survey sample consisted of 1,203 graduates of the University of California at Santa Barbara. To the extent that attitudes and opinions of a small, select population of highly educated university graduates indicate general attitudes and opinions, some tentative assumptions concerning the meaning of children in the United States may be made. Chapter 6 points to some conclusions that may be drawn from the survey with respect to why people may want or not want children today, how they regard children, what degree of commitment they may feel to become parents, and what need they might have personally for valuing children beyond consideration of the social need for species perpetuation. General inferences that may be drawn from the research conclude the study.

Notes

1. Richard Boeth, *Newsweek*, March 12, 1973, p. 56.
2. John O'Connor, *New York Times*, Jan. 23, 1973, p. 79.
3. *Newsweek,* March 12, 1973, p. 55.
4. Ibid., p. 57.
5. Edward Grossman, "The Family in the Tube," *World Magazine,* March 13, 1973, p.54

Notes on Historical Attitudes Toward Children

In order to place into historical perspective current American perceptions concerning the meaning of children, I will briefly trace past attitudes toward family and children, from medieval times to the present. Since early immigrants to the United States brought most of their familistic ideology with them from northwestern Europe, I would like to begin with a short review of medieval and Old World attitudes toward children and then look at New World attitudes in the period from the landing of the Pilgrims to roughly 1700. The eighteenth century, which gave Americans political viability as a nation and firmly implanted them as pioneers of a new way of life, will be covered next, and then the nineteenth century, the broad events of which significantly changed attitudes toward familism and child nurture.

I have divided the period from 1900 to the present into three sections: (1) from 1900 to 1940, encompassing the pre–World War I social and economic promise, followed by the devastation of that conflict, and the disillusionments, dislocations, and ersatz euphoria during the arms buildup prior to the outbreak of World War II; (2) from 1940 to 1965, covering the World War II years and the subsequent reverberations affecting attitudes toward family, resulting in the postwar baby boom; and (3) from 1965 to the present, during which time family patterns and notions of familism have been modified by the disillusioning impact of the Vietnam War and the youth rebellions of the '60s.

Medieval and Old World Attitudes Toward Children

According to Philippe Aries,[1] the seventeenth century marks a changing point when the world of children began to be separated from the world of adults. As early as the thirteenth century, however, "childhood" had been "discovered."[2]

During the tenth century, artists were depicting the child as a small adult, and from the fourteenth into the seventeenth centuries the child was still taking part as a little adult in communal games, family rituals, and festivities, without any particular recognition of his immaturity. According to Peter Laslett,[3] as late as 1697 John Locke was prescribing that children as young as three years of age should *work* for some part of each day. Perhaps children did not "count" as children in those times because of the slender chance most of them had for survival; also, perhaps they were shown as nondescript miniature adults because artists — doubtless under parental directive — simply did not want to trouble with them until they became sufficiently adult to insure a fair chance of survival. To a degree, of course, artists did not bother with them much because, as with all children in all times, they must have been very unreliable sitters. One theory, mentioned by Stephen Brobeck, who has written about American family behavior for the period from 1730 to 1860, suggests that people wanted progeny to be remembered as fully formed adults, hence real likenesses or portraits were deferred until adulthood. Remarking on the fact that so few children were included in portraits of the time, he observed that

> Adults were portrayed far more frequently than children. In the course of [our] investigation, well over 1,000 portraits of adults but only 139 of children were observed. One might be tempted to conclude from this data that adults refused to recognize the importance of children, however, there is a more plausible explanation. In most cases, children were probably far more difficult than adults to pose. Just persuading infants to sit quietly for fifteen minutes while they were sketched may well have taxed the patience of both artist and parent. . . . More important, many parents probably commissioned portraits of themselves but not of their children because they wished future generations to remember them, and their children, as adults.[4]

Certainly, the fact that deceased infants were buried anywhere without ceremony (as we do with dogs and cats)[5] should suggest, perhaps, that children as such had scant meaning for medieval people. (Exempted, of course, were noble heirs.)

Before medical knowledge had advanced to the point of reducing infant mortality, parents did not concentrate on trying to heal sick children. They were commended to heaven, and the thoughts of their parents turned toward sturdier replacements. Also, before the eighteenth century, children were commonly put into the care of wet nurses, at least until they were weaned, a process that in those days might take four or five years.

Although infant mortality stayed high in the seventeenth, eighteenth, and nineteenth centuries, a sensibility was gradually developing toward the potential of children as human beings. During the sixteenth century, paintings with "putti" (naked cherubs in clouds of veils) became prevalent (for example, in Titian's work), indicating a growing interest in children as unique beings. Also, family life had become a subject for artists, and scenes in paintings changed from depictions of impersonal spaces (churches, courtyards, and the like) to intimate interiors (rooms).

From the sixteenth century forward, the child of "quality" began having styles of dress uniquely his own. Although girls' clothing still mimicked that of adult women, boys were less and less dressed as grown men. By the late eighteenth century, boys were put into radically different *effeminate* clothing until they were sometimes nine or ten years old. One might say from this that they were the first *specialized* children. Peasant children of both sexes, of course, wore whatever was handed down to them, but generally it was the same as that worn by adults of the same class. Setting childhood apart began only at the levels of middle class and higher.

Before the seventeenth century, no respect was shown to children under seven years of age; they were often fair game for sexual molestation by adults. They were—if attention was given them at all—little more than playthings. If they survived until seven, however, they did become objects of a certain respect, and to some degree their childhood began to be protected. They were no longer looked upon as unformed adults but as human resources with attributes and capacities valuable to their parents and to society. Such capacities were shaped and made use of in a system of apprenticed household labor that reached into almost every home, even those of the rich. All through the Middle Ages and after, apprenticeship was a way of life for children and the only means of education and training for adulthood. Before the fifteenth century parents cared less about any affection they might have or gain from children than for the contribution the children could make to common tasks. "Family" was a moral, economic, and social reality—not a sentimental one. The following quote by Aries from an account of a fifteenth-century Italian observer regarding treatment of seven to nine-year-olds in England sheds light on medieval indenture practices and attitudes toward children:

> An Italian text of the late fifteenth century gives us an extremely thought-provoking impression of the medieval family, at least in England. It is taken from an account of England by an Italian, [*A Relation of the Island of England,* Camden Society, 1897, p. xiv, quoted in [from] *The Babees Book,* edited by F. J. Furnivall, 1868]: "The want of affection in the English is strongly manifested towards their children; for after having kept them at home till they arrive at the age of seven or nine years at the utmost [in the old French authors, seven is given as the age when the boys leave the care of the womenfolk to go to school or to enter the adult world], they put

them out, both males and females, to hard service in the houses of other people, binding them generally for another seven or nine years [i.e., until they are between fourteen and eighteen]. And these are called apprentices, and during that time they perform all the most menial offices; and few are born who are exempted from this fate, for everyone, however rich he may be, sends away his children into the houses of others, whilst he, in return, receives those of strangers into his own." The Italian considers this custom cruel, which suggests that it was unknown or had been forgotten in his country. He insinuates that the English took in other people's children because they thought that in that way they would obtain better service than they would from their own offspring. In fact the explanation which the English themselves gave to the Italian observer was probably the real one: "In order that their children might learn better manners."[6]

Between the seventeenth and the late nineteenth centuries, the First Communion ceremony became "the most visible manifestation of the idea of childhood."[7] It celebrated both "innocence of childhood . . . and rational appreciation of the sacred mysteries."[8] The rise of schooling coincided. The child was educated in manners and away from ignorance toward reason.

By the fifteenth century, as colleges came into being, new emphasis on permanent buildings, special supervised studies, and regulated life patterns all indicated concern and concentration on the importance of childhood and youth. Weakness and lack of moral formation of the child was recognized. At the end of the sixteenth century, Jesuits instituted strict semimilitary separation of the young male and emphasized moral training. In the seventeenth century the University of Paris was reformed to compete with the Jesuits. Academies for some of the male nobility became prevalent. Parents, recognizing the importance of offspring as private resources, used such institutions to help maintain control of adolescent males until they were ready for the duties of adulthood. Midway through the seventeenth century, the Ursulines began teaching girls of "quality" writing and dealing with household accounts. Prior to that it was unsafe for them to attend schools.

To be sure, all of this attention and schooling was unavailable to the lower classes. Even into the twentieth century lower-class children were channeled into manual labor, excluded from all but elementary classes, and sent to trade schools that would most quickly fit them for work in the labor force.

Attitudes from 1620 to 1700 in the New World

Edmund S. Morgan rightly observes that Puritan parents in the United

States lived with the threat of losing their children's salvation (and the material prosperity of the family if they didn't effect their offsprings' salvation).[9] People's whole lives and their attitudes toward themselves and their children were bound up in the ferocious theology of John Calvin (1509–1564), which postulated total human depravity, the implacable wrath of God, absolute predestination, election of the chosen few, and damnation for the rest.[10] Through the conversion of the parents, children were potentially among the chosen by having been included in the covenant dating back to Abraham; however, it was the duty of parents to educate their children for God. The belief was implacably held that a child came into the world with an inherently corrupt nature, that he had to be "broken," his will "beat" toward the good. He had to be "saved"; consequently he was made to confess his "sins" at an early age.[11] Since children, however, were thought to be corrigible though wicked, strict and prolonged discipline from infancy was considered obligatory lest the Devil get them and the family come to harm. Forcing morality on a group (e.g., the family) was believed to insure protection and outward prosperity.[12]

Church elders made visits to homes to check up on, admonish, censure, or even excommunicate parents remiss in their godly duty toward their children. This kept them constantly vigilant. Any parent showing himself to be a habitual sinner had his children taken from him. Civil authority reinforced family obedience.

Like most parents throughout history, Puritans had concern, however limited, for their progeny, but trained them by instilling fear to gain their respect and obedience. They also used them for material benefit. As we see from Philip Greven's account of colonial Andover, Massachusetts,[13] children well into maturity were bartered in trade-off labor. Parents "loaned out" adolescents, who were not paid for their work; the family received credit in goods or produce for such labor. Thus, children's dependence on parents was prolonged into adulthood, gratuitously resulting, for male heads of households, in the reinforcement of patriarchy. Fathers held out promise of inheritance (of land) to sons, but also at whim could dispose of such land, even if a son and his family lived on it. Thus, even grown children were kept on tenterhooks as to what they might eventually own independently. Few fathers deeded property before their deaths, and even when they did, a provision was usually included that the land would revert to the father if the son did not take care of him in his old age.

In a time of so few alternatives, and when life expectancy was little more than forty-five years,[14] the psychological repercussions must have been severely frustrating if not shattering to young people. One way colonial youth got out of the trap was to emigrate to the wilderness, where with no less uncertainty, perhaps, but with more freedom, they could pioneer new lives of their own.

Attitudes Toward Children in the Eighteenth Century

In the eighteenth century family life in the United States was affected by broad social currents such as the political weakening of religious authority coupled with the erosion of parental authority and disintegration of ties between family and community. The transplanting and flowering of European rationalism, which, along with the new intellectual "enlightenment," embodied growing sexual permissiveness and stylized, artificial attitudes toward love, family, and children also had a major effect on the U.S. family. Ideas of men like John Locke[15] (1632–1704) and Jean Jacques Rousseau[16] (1712–1778) had a strong influence on child nurture as well as on political and social change. Rousseau, particularly, called for a break with the old notion that the child was depraved until redeemed by strictest moralistic disciplining, and stressed the rights children should have as individuals — rights to happiness and love and to respect for their intellectual and emotional development. His *Emile*[17] had great influence on subsequent progressive theories of education. The novel is actually a treatise that sets forth a plan of education to make children morally and intellectually self-reliant, hence well balanced and free. Rousseau also wrote paeans in praise of the purity, modesty, and delicacy of womanhood and motherhood, which foreshadowed what was to happen later to domesticity in the nineteenth century.

Dislocations following the American Revolution and the later repercussions of the French Revolution further confused and disoriented traditional puritanical family values. Toward the end of the eighteenth century, however, rationalism was tempered by a resurgence of Calvinist views that reactivated severely strict disciplining of the young, and early and rigorous religious training. Bernard Wishy observed,

> Despite the prestige and weight we now give the more congenial "modern" ideas of the American Enlightenment, in the very hour of American independence in the 1780's there had begun a remarkable resurgence of Calvinist views and religious conservatism.[18]

Attitudes Toward Children in the Nineteenth Century

During the Jacksonian period of the nineteenth century, concern about children was directly related to the general anxiety and malaise about the state of the nation itself. Moralists bewailed "the 'atheism, licentiousness and intemperance' and the growing lax discipline in the home"[19] as both a retreat from Christian piety and a failure of faith in the moral code of the founders of the republic. What ensued was a burgeoning of new "Christian" ideas of family life, leading to what is referred to as the "cult of domesticity," which developed alongside a widespread push for the reform of child nurture. Citing a work of A. L. Kuhn,[20] Wishy observed,

> The reappraisal of American family life that took place after 1830 brought two conclusions about authority in all types of homes: both fathers and mothers were failing the republic but fathers were neglecting their duties, while mothers were merely inexpert at theirs. The principal emphasis of the nurture writers was for *mothers* to reform themselves in order to accept new and portentous responsibilities. In fact, if we accept and generalize the judgment of one student of New England society in this period, the American mother was now to take the lead in most matters connected with the child.
>
> In the new tide of "domestic reform," the American mother was placed under the sternest pressure. She was to give up wealth, frivolity, and "fashion," to conquer weakness and ailments, sloth and insensitivity, and acquire a discipline and knowledge preparing her for a great calling. The reason was simple enough: the mother was the obvious source of everything that would save or damn the child; the historical and spiritual destiny of America lay in her hands. Her own states of mind, body, and soul were of utmost importance. The "new mother's" place was in the home as the most powerful figure in affecting American society. What were "women's rights" compared with such influence?
>
> By 1840 maternal associations in rural New England were becoming active to help rededication to the holy, healthy hearth.[21]

By mid-century a torrent of popularized treatises that included hortatory tracts, manuals and magazine articles for parents, and moralistic storybook guides for children were published. The publications for parents ranged from the *Works* of Jonathan Edwards, who, a century earlier, had stated flatly that unrepentant children were "young vipers and infinitely more hateful than vipers,"[22] to the writings of Catherine Sedgwick. In her *Home*, affectionate, pliant children were brought to virtue through gentle but implacable psychic control by "an uncompromising father and an all-hoping mother"[23] — and, of course, a heavenly Father. Some other significant publications for the guidance of parents were: *Godey's Lady's Book; The Parent's Magazine; Mother's Magazine;* Jacob Abbott's *The Young Christian;*[24] J.S.C. Abbott's *The Child at Home;*[25] Lydia H. Sigourney's *Letters to Mothers;*[26] and Bronson Alcott's *Observations on the Principles and Methods of Infant Instruction.*[27] Alcott, the father of Louisa M. Alcott, was probably the first child "programmer." He expected nothing less than moral perfection in children, and handled the misbehavior of his three daughters by withdrawal of love and approval, coupled with exaction of repentance and strict obedience.

Among the hundreds of books and periodicals published for children in the last half of the nineteenth century were McGuffey's *Readers,* which according to Glenn Davis[28] reached one hundred million children between 1850 and 1900; Horatio Alger, Jr.'s *Strive and Succeed;*[29] and the *St. Nicholas Magazine.* The inordinate concentration of women's interest at this time in protecting the inviolability of home and family led naturally to campaigns against alcoholism and slavery. These in turn gave vent to suppressed notions of equal rights for women and protective laws to regulate child labor.

Broad social changes brought on by heightened immigration, industrialization, urbanization, western territorial expansion, and particularly by the rending impact of the Civil War and its aftermath, had deeply affected familistic developments, particularly child-rearing practices. As a result of such alienating social forces, people had begun more and more to focus attention on the home as a bulwark against the harsh realities of the swiftly changing "outside" world. Christopher Lasch observed, "As an institution defined above all as a refuge, a private retreat, the family became the center of a new kind of emotional life, a new intimacy and inwardness."[30]

Meanwhile, mid-Victorian morality (Victoria was crowned in 1837) with its near inhuman discipline and repression and its forced determination to reconcile the pursuit of profit with fundamentalist Christianity, was being severely challenged by Darwinism (*The Origin of the Species* was published in 1859) and by the swiftly expanding materialistic machine age. MacIntyre suggested that Western man is unable to discard Christianity, yet finds it difficult to reconcile Christian tenets with secular life. Paraphrasing Engels, he said,

> Engels thought that the secularization of the modern world would take place not merely because belief in Christianity was incompatible with the technical and social processes of industrial society, but because he believed that the technical and social processes of the Industrial Revolution society would in fact bring about a new secular set of beliefs in terms of which men would be able to understand themselves and their society and to control their own future.[31]

He felt Engels was mistaken about this and also about the fact that the inability of men to discard Christianity was part of their inability to provide any post-Christian means of understanding their situation in the world. He added,

> We stand in some danger of falling between those who, on the one hand, hold that human historical change, the change in the ability of men to understand themselves, must be essentially unpredictable and cannot become a matter of science, and those, on the other hand, who hold that it is all a matter for manipulative technique.[32]

Victorian influence persisted long after World War I, in spite of the fact that the war was a cataclysm that changed the face of the world, not only for the decadent political empires of the Old World but also for the United States, a nation that had risen from the travail with the sobering necessity of proving that it was in *fact* what it had become in *symbol*—the last great hope of the future for all men.

The Period from 1900 to 1940

Although based on a century of accelerated social changes resulting from industrial and scientific revolutions, the period from 1900 to roughly the beginning of World War II encompassed even more swiftly won technological transformations and devastating explosions of man's accumulated energies, which he was morally and psychologically unprepared to control. Barbara Tuchman, describing our plight at the beginning of the twentieth century, observed,

> [Man] entered the Twentieth with his capacities in transportation, communication, production, manufacture and weaponry multiplied a thousand fold by the energy of machines. Industrial society gave man new powers and new scope while at the same time building up new pressures in prosperity and poverty, in growth of population and crowding in cities, in antagonisms of classes and groups, in separation from nature and from satisfaction in individual work. Science gave man new welfare and new horizons while it took away belief in God and certainty in a scheme of things he knew. By the time he left the Nineteenth Century he had as much new unease as ease. Although *fin de siècle* usually connotes decadence, in fact society at the turn of the century was not so much decaying as bursting with new tensions and accumulated energies.[33]

The science and technology being discovered and developed at the turn of the century, much of which had been interrupted by World War I and the resulting decimation of talent, was vigorously resumed and expanded in the '20s. The juggernaut of technology was off again and accelerating at an exponential rate. *The New Encylopaedia Britannica* summed up the technological thrust in this way: "What is new in the 20th Century is the magnification of all the predicaments [that antedated 1914] and the blinding concentration on details."[34]

Prominent among significant theoretical developments were relativity and quantum physics. Among the more immediate practical applications were advancements in médicine (asepsis in surgery, x-rays, psychiatry, psychoanalysis), the factory assembly line (automobiles), railroads, embryonic electronic media (notably the telephone, radio, and motion pictures), and, as well, important social advancements such as child labor laws and labor unions. In spite of swift and startling innovations, however, the "neo-decadent" period between the world wars hurtled on toward the global chaos of the 1929 financial crash and the Great Depression.

The growing power of the public schools in U.S. society during the first third of the twentieth century began rapidly to infringe upon the rights of parents to direct the upbringing of their own children, particularly their formal education. This was not done without their consent and cooperation. In the accelerating pace of social and technological expansion, parents gradually began to allow their function as educators to be taken over by institutions outside the family.

The influence of the progressive education of John Dewey led to experimental schools, the philosophy of which embraced the idea that "society should be interpreted to the child through his daily living in the classroom which acts as a miniature society."[35] He believed that "education *is* life and not merely a preparation for life."[36]

Dewey and other education reformers like Jean Piaget and Alfred N. Whitehead had substantial influence on U.S. public school systems and their subsequent usurpation of parental disciplinary prerogatives. Education for citizenship, a strong tenet in their philosophies, was to be attained through the child's actual experience as an individual. Dewey's educational standard required "saturating [the child] with the spirit of service and providing him with the instruments of effective self-direction. . . . The school itself," he said, "shall be made a genuine form of active community life, instead of a place set apart in which to learn lessons."[37]

The Period from 1940 to 1965

The mood of the nation after World War I was to a high degree antifamilistic (Havelock Ellis and Margaret Sanger were at the height of their crusade for contraception) and generally pessimistic and hedonistic following the failure of the League of Nations and the destruction of the American dream of "splendid military isolation." However, the disruption and moral disquiet of post-World War II triggered a strong nostalgia for personal securities deemed lost, evidenced by a mass predilection for familial togetherness. At the core of the new American dream, for returning veterans as well as for other marriageable youth, was a home in suburbia full of healthy, lovable children, situated within commuting distance of a reasonably adequate job for the breadwinner.

The baby boom that resulted exploded without much public notice but had substantial demographic repercussions later, and even today is disruptive of political and economic calculations. As yet unevaluated are some of the subtler ramifications, such as a possible relationship between the togetherness motherhood of the '50s and the prevalence of alcoholism now among women in their forties who have Spock-reared teenagers.

The Period After 1965

The period from the '60s to the present began with the rise of the adversary youth culture, the main force behind the civil rights movement and the anti-Vietnam crusade. It has been a period of parental confusion and irresolution, of uncertain probing for "modern" ways to reconcile the rightful claims of the child to rebel against tradition and authority, with the rational right of parents to enforce sanctions to limit the child's freedom for his own safety and development. It could be said that for both parents and offspring, the '60s represented a turbulent watershed that, in the experience of tribulations and disillusionments, precipitately separated the complacent, immature societal mood of the '50s from that of the "instant" maturation of the decade that followed. In the '70s, the mood — of the young, at least — changed to one of renewed determination to break with the immediate past and attend to endeavors that would have more stabilizing effects on basic human and planetary commitments.

Max Lerner has called the '60s "scarred and scarring."[38] He reflected that there were two "revolutions" going on during that decade — the activist-political movements and the cultural revolts — and that the cultural changes begun then have been more enduring than the power showdowns that seemed earthshaking ten or fifteen years ago. He suggested that the political fevers have ended, observing that

actually these revolutions fell into two groupings — the activist and the cultural movements of change. One was primarily political, in the realm of rights, equality and power. The other was primarily cultural, in the realm of attitudes, ideas, values, morals, codes . . . the impact of the cultural movements has proved more enduring than the political.[39]

Noting that there were erotic elements in all the activist movements, he said,

> The youngsters who fought together in the demonstrations, and slept together during the stretches between them, found that danger was more attractive because of the pang of the erotic, and that sex took on more excitement from the edge of danger. Rock music and drugs intensified the power contests. The sense of the toppling of value systems and the feeling of code-breaking and code-making were experiences to be renewed and relived even when the chants of demonstrators and the sound of police sirens had grown dim.[40]

He added that the "scarred and scarring 60's have been succeeded by the sober 70's."[41] Indeed, the focus in the '70s turned toward environmentalism, self-fulfillment, and the fear of global nuclear annihilation. There has been a groping among the young (and the not so young) for new forms of familism with a basic structure of commitment that will accommodate within its framework the realities of contemporary marital experimentation involving premarital cohabitation, single parenthood, the melding of new families from broken marriages, and shared child custody.

Notes

1. Philippe Aries, *Centuries of Childhood: A Social History of Family Life* (New York: Alfred A. Knopf, 1962).

2. See for example, the works on childhood and child care of Bernard de Gordon, *Regimen sanitatis* (1200?), and Michele Savonarola, *Practica de egritudinibus* (1486), as discussed in Luke Demaitre's "The Idea of Childhood and Child Care in Medical Writings of the Middle Ages," *Journal of Psychohistory* 4, no. 4 (Spring 1977).

3. Peter Laslett, *The World We Have Lost: England Before the Industrial Age*, 2nd ed. (New York: Charles Scribner's Sons, 1971), p. 3.

4. Stephen Brobeck, "Images of the Family: Portrait Paintings as Indices of American Family Culture, Structure and Behavior, 1730-1860," *The Journal of Psychohistory* 5, no. 1 (Summer 1977): 84-85.

5. Aries, *Centuries of Childhood*, p. 39.

6. Ibid., pp. 365, 435.

7. Ibid., p. 127.

8. Ibid.

9. Edmund S. Morgan, *The Puritan Family: Religion and Domestic Relations in Seventeenth-Century New England* (New York: Harper Torchbooks, Academy Library, 1966).

10. Morton M. Hunt, *The Natural History of Love* (New York: Alfred A. Knopf, 1959), p. 225

11. John Demos, "The American Family in Past Time," *The American Scholar* (Summer 1974).

12. Morgan, *The Puritan Family*, p. 10.

13. Philip Greven, Jr., *Four Generations: Population, Land and Family in Colonial Andover, Massachusetts* (Ithaca, N.Y.: Cornell University Press, 1970).

14. Laslett, *The World We Have Lost*, p. 288, cites John Demos' figure of 45.5 as being too high.The figure for women alone was considerably lower due to the hazards of childbirth. In the seventeenth century one could not with confidence expect to see one's grandchildren. In the words of Laslett, "The society of the preindustrial world was inured to bereavement and shortness of life" (p. 100).

15. See *The New Encyclopaedia Britannica*, 15th ed. (Chicago: 1974), Macropaedia, vol. 8, p. 1136d, and vol. 13, p. 1100e. See also *John Locke, Concerning the True Original Extent and End of Civil Government* (Chicago: Great Books of the Western World, 1937), vol. 35, chap. 6, pp. 36–42.

16. See *The New Encyclopaedia Britannica*, Macropaedia, vol. 6, pp. 353–354; and vol. 13, pp. 1100d and 359f.

17. Jean Jacques Rousseau, *Emilius, or a Treatise of Education*, vols. 1-3, translated from the French of J. J. Rousseau (Edinburgh: W. Coke, Bookseller in Leith, 1773) [*Emile* (1762)].

18. Bernard Wishy, *The Child and the Republic* (Philadelphia: University of Pennsylvania Press, 1968), p. 12.

19. Ibid.

20. A. L. Kuhn, *The Mother's Role in Childhood Education* (New Haven, Conn.: Yale University Press, 1947).

21. Wishy, *Child and Republic*, p. 28.

22. As quoted by Wishy, ibid., p. 11.

23. Catherine Sedgwick, *Home* (Boston: James Munroe and Company, 1835), p. 18.

24. Jacob Abbott, *The Young Christian* (New York, 1851).

25. J.S.C. Abbott, *The Child at Home* (New York, 1833).

26. Lydia H. Sigourney, *Letters to Mothers* (Hartford, 1838).

27. Bronson Alcott, *Observations on the Principles and Methods of Infant Instruction* (Boston, 1830).

28. Glenn Davis, *Childhood and History in America* (New York: The Psychohistory Press, 1976), p. 48.

29. Horatio Alger, Jr., *Strive and Succeed* (Chicago: M. A. Donohue, 1872).

30. Christopher Lasch, *The New York Review of Books*, Nov. 27, 1975, p. 40.

31. Alasdair MacIntyre, *Secularization and Moral Change* (London: Oxford University Press, 1967), p. 75.

32. Ibid., p. 76.

33. Barbara Tuchman, *The Proud Tower* (New York: Macmillan, 1966), pp. xiv-xv.

34. *The New Encyclopaedia Britannica*, Macropaedia, vol. 6, p. 1080.

35. Ibid., p. 374g.

36. Ibid.

37. John Dewey, *The School and Society*, Revised ed. (Chicago: University of Chicago Press, 1915), pp. 27–28.

38. Max Lerner, "The Scarred 60's and the Sober 70's," *Santa Barbara News Press*, December 14, 1977, p. F-12.

39. Ibid.

40. Ibid.

41. Ibid.

3
Contemporary Trends Affecting the Meaning of Children

Today, a multitude of interacting concordant and also conflicting elements widely and deeply affect the meaning and purpose of all human activity, especially that related to bearing and rearing children. At the crucial core is the poignant failure of both religion and family to be, as in the past, "the mighty fortress" against all vicissitudes, more specifically against the threats to stability and well-being that are generated by the complexity and seeming frenzy of our technotronic society.

Carle C. Zimmerman described as "atomistic" the contemporary period, in which the individual is freed of family bonds and the state becomes much more an organization of individuals. "In atomistic periods," he said, "the family seems unimportant and the whole culture takes on an individualistic coloration."[1] He added, "All of society, from the writers of family books on down, have ideas which fundamentally place the individual rampantly above the family."[2]

Zimmerman's comment in 1947 on familism and the decay of western civilization is noteworthy for its validity in predicting continuing trends:

> The western world has entered a period of demoralization comparable to the periods when both Greece and Rome turned from growth to decay. Divorce, premarital sex experience, sex promiscuity, homosexuality, versatility in sex, birth control carried to excess, spread of birth control to every segment of the population, positive antagonism to parenthood, clandestine marriage, migratory divorce, marriage for sex alone, contempt for familism, even in the so-called educated circles—all are increasing rapidly. In spite of our virtuous words, and without even the intellectual honesty of the Greeks and Romans, we have gone as far as they, and it would appear that we are going even farther. The family crisis of the nineteenth and twentieth centuries is like that in Greece and Rome, except that we do not recognize it and are intellectually dishonest with ourselves on this subject."[3]

Compared to any former times, of course, there is less and less mystery about the phenomena of nature affecting man, due in large part to the cultural supremacy of scientific and technological knowledge. Religious beliefs and proscriptions, notably those relating to the sacredness of the family, have been demythologized, and desacralized.[4] The earlier strong interconnection that existed between religion and social organization, especially with respect to familial activities, has all but vanished. With the hegemony of scientific certainties and the spread of secularization into all areas of contemporary life, the fear of metaphysical sanctions that once kept the idea of family rigid and inviolable has almost totally dissipated. In its place has come the belief that, if there is any religious necessity for men, guidance must be sought by people as individuals.

It cannot be too strongly emphasized that as far as individual personal values and behavior are concerned, U.S. society has become highly pluralistic. There is a lack of shared moral vocabulary. Authoritative moral dicta are no longer applicable,[5] least of all when they stem from another age. The absence of a basic consensus on moral values[6] tends to alienate[7] and "de-group" people, and diverse, individualistic family patterns allow for wide and casual acceptance of nonconformance with what, nevertheless, is known to be the traditional norm. What is still traditionally regarded as normal, however, no longer serves as a legitimated model for the whole society. Variances from the norm are less and less viewed to be deviations. There is more room today for diversity of living situations and values, and there are more choices more easily obtained than ever before.

Although nonconformity to the vaguely known general norm in mating patterns incurs few if any open sanctions today, deep-seated frustrations connected with breaking new ground in sexual patterns intensify current general alienations. This applies particularly to couples cohabiting outside marriage, to "swingers," and to homosexuals. J. Richard Udry observed, "A nonconformist orientation to marriage and family life makes life interesting. It is also continuously frustrating and by definition subject to social punishment at every turn. Most couples cannot take this very long."[8] In spite of the trends, a conservative majority persists with gut-reaction prejudices that are rooted in past traditions and the social contexts of individual childhood experiences, and this majority does exert considerable social control.[9]

One of the more notable influences affecting family values and attitudes toward rearing children in the United States today is the continuing proliferation of large formal public and private bureaucratic organizations in which everybody spends a great deal of time *away* from family. Such institutions affect all areas of life, including schooling, work, recreation, amateur and professional sports, and other avocational activities, and they have much to do with decisions and control of the social as well as the economic, educative, and recreational functions of the family. Many of the former functions of the family (such as schooling, health care, and recreation) have long since been taken over — in part, at least — by such bureaucratic institutions.[10] These latter frequently are not fulfilling these tasks very well,[11] hence expectations linger that the contemporary family, shorn as it is of important societal functions — and out of practice to perform them — should somehow be made to do all the things it used to do for people, plus others spawned by the complexities of contemporary life. The sober fact is that because of disuse of its potentialities, the American family has atrophied to little more than a place to hang one's hat — though, to be sure, it is still the prime locus for procreation and child personality formation.

The vast self-perpetuating welfare system, which forces men to desert their families in order to qualify them for government support and thereby encourages dependence that lasts for generations, can have only negative effects on both the attitudes welfare recipients have about their children and on incentives for their children to make better lives for themselves.

To a marked extent, family entertainment has gone out of the home and neighborhood and has become largely a spectator activity primarily for the individual. (Who can remember familial "sings" around the piano, taffy pulls, quilting bees, and barn raisings?) Of course, television, radio, stereo, and other electronic artifacts have brought people back into the house to a degree — not as family units, but rather as gatherings of individuals. The social focus has shifted from home to places of work, play, and the like.[12]

The general mobility of the populace, while affording wide-ranging opportunities never before available, has also reinforced feelings of rootlessness. Certainly, the mobility incidental to frequent and arbitrary job transfers by employers of breadwinners leads to familial life-styles of impermanence and instability. For slum dwellers, such as those in the "airtight cage"[13] of Harlem, for example, the mobility of others, unattainable for them, serves only to aggravate their frustrations. The enormous problems of overurbanization and crowding that have resulted in the decay of inner cities, and the apparent inability of federal, state and municipal governments to effect any timely amelioration, have markedly affected familial attitudes of all citizens, especially those living in and near such areas — be they poor or otherwise.

Coupled with mobility as a disorienting factor is the fragmented and frenetic quality life has today in all areas of activity.[14] The hectic tempo allows no time for people to *enjoy one another*; parents, in particular, are hard pressed to find time and energy to really enjoy their children.

Although the birth rate in the United States has declined in recent years, owing in part to the easy accessibility and widespread acceptance of contraception and abortion, as well as to the need or desire of women to work outside the home and not have children, the statistics for January through May 1977 show a slight increase in birth rate vis-à-vis the same period in 1976. Contributing to the turnabout is a persistent and disturbing increase in teenage pregnancies.[15] Also, currently across all childbearing ages there is what may be a temporary "echo" baby boom, resulting from the fact that girls born in the postwar baby boom are now passing through their prime years of fertility. The following excerpt from *Science News* gives pertinent details on recent fertility trends:

The fertility rate for the first third of this year [1977] was 68.4 children per 1,000 women of childbearing age (15 to 44) . . . an increase of 5 percent over a comparable span in 1976. . . . However, the current rate of 1.84 children per woman is still below the "replacement level" of 2.1 children for American society.

While a birth-rate increase would be welcomed by those who fear that prolonged zero population growth would some day produce a geriatric society, there is at least one aspect of the rising trend that bothers even proponents: teenage pregnancies. That problem has been steadily growing during the last few years. . . . More than one million 15 to 19 years olds a year get pregnant in America. More than half the 21 million persons in that age range have sexual intercourse. . . . Of those who get pregnant, 28 percent are married before conception takes place, 21 percent give birth out of wedlock, 14 percent have miscarriages and 27 percent have abortions.

University of Michigan psychologist Sylvia S. Hacker traces much of the teenage problem to lack of proper use of contraceptives, caused ultimately by inadequate sex education. . . . Despite the advent of academic sex education, boys and girls remain "uneasy or uninformed about sex. Sex education classes in this country . . . are dealing with anatomy and reproduction when what kids really want to know about are human relationships — 'What will she think if I try something,' or 'How far should I let him go?'" The more uneasy or uninformed a boy or girl feels about sex, the less likely they are to use birth control. . . . "Sex and contraception are still relatively taboo subjects in our post-Puritanical culture," she says. "Even the most liberal parents tend to view sex as a private matter, and the schools treat it as a dry academic subject."

For whatever reasons, teenagers and adults alike are contributing to the current upswing in births. Whether or not this marks the start of a new baby boom remains to be seen.[16]

It may be noted that other researchers in the field also see signs of a philosophical return to the traditional marriage concept. Yet anthropologist Margaret Mead warned, "When both sexes [in a society] set their hearts against reproduction, then such societies die out—even without benefit of contraception."[17] Certainly, wide acceptance of birth control in contemporary customs has radically changed attitudes about the necessity or desirability of having more than a minimal number of children—or, in fact, any at all.

A recent Bureau of the Census report of statistics to March 1976 commented on the rise in *two*-person households:

> More than half of all households in the country contain only one or two persons. Low fertility, postponement of marriage, the formation of households by those born during the baby boom, the ability of young singles and the elderly to finance and maintain their own households, and marital dissolution are all contributors to the increase in households containing no more than two people.[18]

Regarding *single* nonfamily households, the same report stated, "There were more than twice as many one-person households in 1976 as in 1960. . . . The share of all households occupied by people living alone has increased from 13.1 to 20.6 percent since 1960."[19]

During the seven years from 1970 to 1978, the number of men living alone rose 60 percent, and the number of single women living alone was up 35 percent. Significantly, persons of retirement age accounted for 42 percent of those living alone in 1977. Yet, the number of single male householders under the age of twenty-five tripled since 1970 and the number of women in the same age category doubled. This finding indicates a diminishing interest in traditional family life and may appreciably affect U.S. demographic findings in the future. No doubt the trend also reflects both the financial ability of singles to maintain households and their instinctive quest for privacy in a world that is "too much with us." It may also reflect the choice of many young people to delay marriage, which in many cases means also postponing childbearing past the point of possibility or desirability.

The ego appeal of perpetuating the family name, genes, status, and the like is still present but has waned appreciably in a depersonalized "throwaway" society. The achievement of personal immortality through one's children is no longer a goal, or even a subject of platitude. Indeed, immortality itself as a personal spiritual goal appears to have been downgraded to a childish myth. Even the role of motherhood has lost much of its appeal as a model for growing daughters.

Although the rate of divorce in the United States showed no increase for the first third of 1977,[20] the total number of divorces per year has continued to rise over a long period. Recently enacted no-fault divorce laws make dissolution of marriage relatively easy. (The very designation "dissolution of marriage" instead of "divorce" lessens the stigma that had already become minimal in the recent past.) Soaring suicide rates, particularly among the young, also contribute to the general apprehensiveness about bearing and rearing children.

Still another factor is child abuse. An alarming rise in violence toward children in the home has occurred, and methods of deterrence or control are inadequate or not yet widely effectual, either on the part of public authorities or the guilty individuals themselves — even though in many cases the latter recognize their incapacity to handle the problem and seek outside professional help. As has been the case through the centuries, not all people are cut out to be parents, but today a substantial percentage of the child batterers are themselves hardly more than children and ill prepared by either tradition or training for the responsibilities of parenthood — least of all in an unstable and alienating society. Dr. Karl Menninger, noting that violence to children has helped breed the violence around us, called attention to a broader societal concern, "The older generation, to some extent is reaping what it sowed. Children do what they were taught by their parents . . . what's done to children, they will do to society."[21]

People who yearn for the return of the "extended family" should take note of its surreptitious — and perhaps *unacceptable* — functional reemergence by way of the complicated webs of child nurture that are present or developing due to multiparenting by the divorced. Given contemporary serial marriage, it is not unusual for children to have two or more sets of "parents." Additionally, a child can have three generational families, at least temporarily, when, for example, a divorced woman returns with her offspring to her mother (or to the family of her origin). Even mate-sharing "swinger" parents are providing forms of the extended family. As James and Lynn Smith observed, "It seems likely that for an increasing proportion of couples involved in co-marital sex, the swingers' 'network' is becoming a functional equivalent for the modified extended family."[22]

Today, fewer young people, in college or out, have any long-range plans for their lives. The prevailing mood is to have short-term commitments, to "live as you go." The uncertainties of the nation's economic outlook may be primarily responsible for this attitude. Unquestionably, unrelieved inflation and unemployment have a deterring effect on planning a life's work. The ecological crisis, also national (and now global) in scope, arising out of the pollution of land, air, oceans, and streams by nuclear wastes, oil, and other industrial effluents, has profoundly affected the idealism of the young. Inescapably dissuasive also are the violence in the media and on the streets; the widespread use of illegal drugs and alcohol; the debilitating effects of acid and punk rock; and Watergate and the scandal of South Korea influence-buying from U.S. congressmen (which have undermined regard for public officials as models for the young). And perhaps most important are the shame of Vietnam, current senseless international terrorism, and the almost unimpeded buildup of nuclear and other arms that may well lead to a third world war and the end of our present civilization. Certainly, these give young people little reason to hope for opportunity in the future. Large-scale student rebellions may be over for now, but the seeds remain.[23]

In this time of broadening tendencies toward individualism, parents themselves are coming to realize and to assert that they too have needs that are as important as those of children. And, given the relaxation of societal pressures to conform, these needs of parents as *individuals* cannot be denied.

Parents are becoming more aware that adults as well as children have capacities for continuing development as separate persons. In former times, adulthood was considered to be fixed state, a cutoff place beyond which a person did not usually seek further personal development or education. Now the watchphrases are "continuing education," "life-long learning"[24] and the like. Ordinary people, better informed about available opportunities by the mass media as well as by various kinds of public relations agencies such as those associated with community educational organizations, realize that it is never too late to learn, and that generally speaking, a person in this country today can continue to develop new skills and capacities that will yield new personal advancement and satisfactions. Medical and psychological authorities emphasize not only the ability of aging minds to absorb and create but also the salutary effects of such efforts. Moreover, educative opportunities for adults abound in almost every community, even small ones, and national television networks are increasingly orienting programs in that direction. Numerous "human potential" movements, such as transcendental meditation and the self-awareness groupings adhering to teachings of people such as the late Abraham Maslow, contribute to the yearning for individual self-development and self-expression.

Too, parents are beginning to understand that responsibility for the mental health of their children no longer rests solely with them. Influences outside the home (for example, bureaucratized technology) are both coculpable for any aberrations and coresponsible for redress (by way of public institutions—both preventive and curative). Of course, parents have complete legal responsibility for their minor children; however, since institutions such as courts and health, education, and welfare organizations have usurped many of the functions of the family, parents exercise only partial authority over their children. Thus, parents everywhere have lost faith in their own ability to rear their children properly. No longer are parents judged by their peers, against whom people once felt qualified to argue their convictions. Instead, they are judged by the experts—professional psychologists, family counselors, and the like—who often are intimidating and prove as well to be questionable substitutes for native parental intelligence and intuition.

With women's realization that they no longer have to bear the total burden of nurturing and forming their children in early childhood (and do not have to bear children at all if they do not want them) has come a trend toward "androgynous" parenthood wherein the father is expected to share the burden of child nurture and training as well as the act of generation and economic support. Such awareness on the part of women has been one of the results of the "consciousness-raising" efforts of the women's liberation movement.

Norman Podhoretz offered a new insight into the significance of the women's liberation movement in terms of a woman's need or desire for children. Commenting on the "feminization of America" (as contrasted to its "greening" or "bluing"), he feared that women, through their drive for individual success, were promoting a new worship of that "bitch-goddess Success" that William James at the turn of the century called "our national disease."[25]

Noting the reluctance of the children of blue-collar families to replace on the success ladder the uppermiddle class children of the 1960s who had grown contemptuous of the idea of success, Podhoretz observed,

As we know now, this "bluing of America" did not occur. Instead, we witnessed an analogous process that might be called the feminization of America, in which young women full of drive and the ambition for success emerged to take the place of all those young men who had gone off in a drug-induced stupor to the hills of Vermont or the streets of San Francisco.

Having discovered themselves to be an oppressed group, these women were able to secure the same exemption from the taboo against the ambition for success that had previously been granted to the blacks. Unlike the blacks, however, they were as ferocious and unrestricted in their expression of the desire to "make it in a man's world" as the most orthodox devotees of the bitch-goddess in the days of William James.

What seems to be happening now is a spillover of influence back into the general culture: success having once again been legitimized by women, it can now be pursued wholeheartedly even by men. *My guess is that this contribution to the legitimation of success may in the long run turn out to be the single most fateful consequence of the women's movement for American life.* [Italics added.][26]

If women are leading the relegitimizing of feverish pursuit of careers "within the system," the effect of this development upon the meaning of children and where children may or may not fit into the societal picture for the future may, indeed, be significant.

Although in some cases children may be used as antidotes to rootlessness, in others they are considered to be unaffordable luxuries owing to the uncertain economic situation, joblessness, and the ever-inflating cost of living. Contributing to the high cost, of course, are the compulsions of consumerism and installment buying, which have long been the framework of U.S. economic policy. John Kenneth Galbraith went so far as to state that in the U.S. economy, happiness is a function of the supply of goods and services consumed (powerfully reinforced by advertising and salesmanship) and that housewives in their "crypto-servant" role as administrators and managers of the buying make an indefinitely increasing consumption possible.[27]

Ivan Illich had the following to say about consumerism and the relegation of individual action to institutions:

> The myth of unending consumption has taken the place of the belief in the life everlasting. We demand everything because we've been trained to expect that anything we can visualize can be supplied by some institution. If atomic waste is poisoning us, today, don't worry because *somehow* we'll find an answer tomorrow. And, of course, the answers will be found through giant institutions, because we have accepted a paralysis of human action at the community level, convinced that family and community are no longer capable of solving problems in a shared manner.[28]

Notes

1. Carle C. Zimmerman, *Family and Civilization* (New York: Harper & Brothers, 1947), p. 694.
2. Ibid., p. 632.
3. Ibid.
4. See William F. Ogburn and Meyer F. Nimkoff, *Sociology* (Boston: Houghton Mifflin Co., 1950), esp. p. 451: "The forms of religious belief have always been linked with the state of knowledge."
5. See Alasdair MacIntyre, *Secularization and Moral Change* (New York: Ox-

ford University Press, 1967), p. 53: "Unless there is an established and shared right way of doing things, so that we have social agreement on how to follow the rules and how to legislate about them, the notion of authority in morals is empty." Also, "In our society, the notion of moral authority is no longer a viable one."

6. See Thomas C. Reeves, "Religion and Reformers," *The Living Church* (June 5, 1977), esp. p. 10: "Beyond almost all of the problems that plague us is the perilous absence of any significant authority of moral and ethical standards." See also, Peter L. Berger, *The Sacred Canopy: Elements of a Sociological Theory of Religion* (New York: Doubleday & Co., 1967), p. 125: "Probably for the first time in history, the religious legitimations of the world have lost their plausibility, not only for a few intellectuals and other marginal individuals, but for broad masses of entire societies."

7. "Men first of all lost any over-all social agreement as to the right ways to live together, and so ceased to be able to make sense of any claims to moral authority." MacIntyre, *Secularization and Moral Change*, p. 54.

8. J. Richard Udry, *The Social Contract of Marriage*, 2nd ed. (Philadelphia: J. B. Lippincott Co., 1971), p. 21.

9. Consider Anita Bryant's campaign against homosexuality, which defeated a prohomosexuality measure in New York, and the strength of Phyllis Schlafly's efforts against feminists and the Equal Rights Amendment.

10. See Zimmerman, *Family and Civilization*, p. 701. Referring to Ogburn's view of family functions as "affectional, procreative, economic, educational, protective, and religious," Zimmerman cites Ogburn's theory that the last four functions have been taken over by the state or the community. "If we take Ogburn's theory and rephrase it, the decay of family functions is associated with a decay in the family. His statistics simply prove that allegiance to family values and processes disappears as more and more of the people have few or no children. Since the functions of the family depend upon having a family, a decrease in those functions does not mean a new type of family but that fewer and fewer of the people become immersed in a full familistic system of values."

11. See Ivan Illich, *Deschooling Society* (New York: Harper & Row, 1971), and *Medical Nemesis: The Expropriation of Health* (London: Calder & Boyars, Ltd., 1975).

12. Edith de Rham, *The Love Fraud* (New York: Clarkson N. Potter, Inc., 1965), saw people as having become "highly evolved gypsies." She said that what is lost is more than a sense of permanence—it is a sense of *place* that is home; that there has been a shift of focus from home to factory, office, places of play, and entertainment; and that even our houses are not planned and constructed for permanence (i.e., through generations) (p. 94).

13. Joseph P. Lyford, *The Airtight Cage* (New York: Harper & Row, 1966).

14. Steffan B. Linder, *The Harried Leisure Class* (New York: Columbia University Press, 1970), quoted Erich Fromm: "For modern man, patience is as difficult to practice as discipline and concentration. Our whole industrial system fosters exactly the opposite: quickness" (p. 92). Also, "our culture leads to an unconcentrated and diffused mode of life, hardly paralleled anywhere else. You do

so many things at once; you read, listen to the radio, talk, smoke, eat, drink. You are the consumer with the open mouth, eager, and ready to swallow everything" (p. 100). Richard Ballad, "The Testimony of Ivan Illich," *Human Behavior* (Feb. 1977), quoted Illich: "It is one of the terrible ironies of history that rich America is now the most *disadvantaged* nation, because it cannot envisage a true alternative to the unbridled use of technology and mad consumption. You are going so fast you can't stop!" (p. 26).

15. National Center for Health Statistics, *Vital Statistics Report*, vol. 26, no. 5 (Aug. 10, 1977), stated: "The birth rate [from Jan. through May 1977] was 15.0 compared with 14.1 for the corresponding period in 1976" (p. 1). Also *Vital Statistics Report*, vol. 25, no. 10 (Dec. 30, 1976): "The illegitimacy rate for teenagers continued to increase in 1975 (4 percent)" (p. 4).

16. "Babies Bottom Out — a 'Maybe Boom,'" *Science News* (Aug. 13, 1977), p. 101.

17. Margaret Mead, *Male and Female* (New York: William Morrow & Co., 1968), p. 238.

18. U.S. Department of Commerce, Bureau of the Census, Series P-20, no. 311, "Population Characteristics," Aug. 1977.

19. Ibid.

20. According to *Vital Statistics Report*, "The divorce rate for the period was the same in both years [1976 and 1977 — 5.0 per 1,000 population]" (vol. 26, no. 5, Aug. 10, 1977). "The [1975] national divorce rate was 4.9 per 1,000 population, the highest annual divorce rate ever observed for this country. . . . Provisional data indicate a further increase to a rate of 5.0 for 1976" (vol. 26, no. 2, May 19, 1977). "The number of divorces . . . has more than doubled from 1966 to 1975" (*Annual Summary* for the U.S. 1975, vol. 24, no. 13, June 30, 1976, p. 12). Another pertinent statistic is the following: "The national estimated number of children under 18 years of age involved in divorce was 1,123,000 in 1975; this is the fourth year with more than 1 million children affected by divorce" (vol. 26, no. 2, May 19, 1977, p. 2).

21. Pam Proctor, "Dr. Karl Menninger Pleads: Stop Beating Your Kids," *Parade* (Oct. 9, 1977): 24-25.

22. James R. Smith and Lynn G. Smith, *Beyond Monogamy* (Baltimore, Md.: Johns Hopkins University Press, 1974), pp. 304-305.

23. Witness the marches and sit-ins connected with antinuclear power crusades, and such sit-ins as the one at the University of California at Davis by demonstrators who were protesting the University's investments in companies doing business in South Africa.

24. Strongly advocated by Robert M. Hutchins, in *The Learning Society* (New York: Praeger Publishers, 1968).

25. Norman Podhoretz, "The Return of Success," *Newsweek* (Aug. 29, 1977), p. 11.

26. Ibid.

27. John Kenneth Galbraith, *Economics and the Public Purpose* (Boston: Houghton Mifflin Company, 1973), ch. 4.

28. Ballad, "The Testimony of Ivan Illich," p. 26.

4
A Survey to Elicit
Contemporary Attitudes

At the beginning of the research project, I posed the following question: What meaning do children have for people in contemporary U.S. society? Particularly, why do people want or not want children today, and what significance might such attitudes have for individuals and for society?

After arriving at some comprehension of historical attitudes toward children, and following a study of contemporary trends affecting the meaning of children, I decided to survey a segment of people in order to elicit existing specific attitudes and opinions about the meaning of children, at least among a given "universe."

I devised a questionnaire (Figure 2) that, in accordance with its cover letter (Figure 1), was intended to elicit "current attitudes toward children, the place of children in the lives of adults today, and especially their meaning for parents." Inherent in the original question of what meaning children have for people in contemporary American society was the hope of discovering specific and perhaps novel reasons for attitudes for and against having children. I wanted to get opinions from parents, from prospective parents, and from declared nonparents, as to reasons for given attitudes. I wanted to determine the degrees to which such attitudes might be (1) egoistic, (2) religious, (3) unconsciously or consciously psychological, (4) economic, and/or (5) other. I wanted to know the degree of commitment or responsibility people now might feel toward society to procreate or not; what basic human "needs" might impel people to want and to have children; and what societal-familial relationships there might be in such needs.

The Sample

The survey began in September 1976 with a universe of 1,200 graduates of the University of California at Santa Barbara (U.C.S.B.), who were heterogeneous as to age but more or less homogeneous as to education and social status. The object was systematically to select 150 men and 150 women from each of four graduating classes, thus arriving at an equal number of males and females in each group of 300 people in the following age categories: A, early 20s; B, late 20s; C, 30s; and D, 50s and older. In order to accomplish this, the following graduation years were tentatively selected: 1975, 1970, 1963, and 1947. Thus, 1947 would include post–World War II graduates; 1963 would have people who upon graduation had not been seriously affected by student uprisings; 1970 would certainly contain people who had been affected by campus unrest and violence; and 1975, the latest graduating class whose names were available in 1976, would contain a large percentage of people as yet unmarried who might be expected to have strong opinions about marriage and childbearing.

For Group D, all U.C.S.B. graduates of the years 1946–1948 were included, since graduates for the three years together totaled only 401. In 1946, there were 24 male and 45 female graduates; in 1947, there were 73 male and 54 female graduates; and in 1948, there were 127 male and 78 female graduates. All totaled, there were 224 male and 177 female graduates. For Group D, therefore, every third male name and every sixth female name were omitted to arrive at a total of 150 of each sex. Additionally, 2 males and 3 females were disregarded at the end of the list.

For Group C, in 1963 there were 155 male and 150 female graduates, for a total of 305. One male and one female foreign student were eliminated, reducing the total to 303. The full total of 154 male and 149 female graduates for 1963 was then used. This slight unavoidable discrepancy produced a total for all groups of 1,203 instead of the round figure of 1,200 that has been used previously for designating the extent of the survey.

For Group B, in 1970 there were 964 male and 807 female graduates for a total of 1,771. Every sixth male name was selected and 10 were deducted at random for a total of 150 men. Every fifth female name was selected and 11 were deducted at random for a total of 150 women. Foreign students, who were few in this group, were not selected but were counted.

For Group A, in 1975 there were 1,495 male and 1,251 female graduates for a total of 2,746. Every tenth male name and every ninth female name plus 11 females selected at random were chosen.

Thus, the four sample groups finally selected were comprised as follows: Group D, 150 males and 150 females from the 1946–1948 classes; Group C, 154 males and 149 females from the 1963 class; Group

B, 150 males and 150 females from the 1970 class; and Group A, 150 males and 150 females from the 1975 class. When the survey was completed, a few adjustments had to be made in order to place respondents in proper categories, due to the fact that in some instances older people were late in graduating, or ages were not given and had to be surmised from the year of graduation. Such discrepancies were few, as indicated below, and do not appreciably distort the findings.

The following, then, were the age groupings and sex distributions used in compiling results of the returned and completed questionnaires:

Group	Age	Male	Female	Total
A	25 and under	39	56	95
B	26 to 31, incl.	63	76 (incl. 1*)	139
C	32 to 44, incl.	65	87 (incl. 2*)	152
D	45 and over	55 (incl. 4*)	84 (incl. 2*)	139
		222	303	525

*Ages not given, surmised by graduation year.

Of the total of 1,203 questionnaires mailed, 47 (22 male and 25 female) were returned undeliverable by the post office. These were not counted in the computation to ascertain percentage of completed returns. Thus, considering 1,156 as the net total questionnaires, and that 525 were completed and returned, over 45 percent of the people returned and answered the questionnaire.

The responses on the questionnaires were counted and analyzed by use of a computer with the help of Hugh Kawabata at the computer center of the University of California at Santa Barbara, resulting in the first instance in frequencies for each group. In computer printouts, groups were designated 1, 2, 3, and 4, instead of A, B, C, and D, respectively. Thus the age groups in the analysis and in the tables are designated by the dual system: A(1), B(2), C(3), and D(4).

Material relevant to opinions and attitudes was cross-tabulated by computer for comparison of all groups. These data will be discussed in Chapter 5.

Descriptive Background of Respondents

Tables 1 through 22 set forth for each age group the salient background framework regarding age, sex, citizenship, ethnicity, marital status, children, composition of household membership, religion, political attitude, education, occupation, working status, personal and family income, and residential pattern.

Age, Sex, Citizenship, Ethnicity

From Table 1 it will be seen that about 58 percent of the respondents were female and 42 percent were male; that all but 2 respondents were U.S. citizens; and that nearly 93 percent classified themselves as Anglo-American.

Marital Status

It is not very surprising that 77 percent of those with an average age of 23 were single and never married, as shown by Table 2, or that only about 7 percent of those with average ages of 35 and 54 never married and were single. It may, however, be of some significance that 33 percent of those with an average age of 28 who answered the question on marital status were also single and never married. As seen in Table 3, of those "now legally married," 21 were in their second marriage — 2 from Group B(2), 9 from Group C(3), and 10 from Group D(4) — and 6 were in their third marriage — 2 from Group C(3) and 4 from Group D(4).

Only 34 people responded as "now divorced" (see questionnaire): 5 in Group B(2), 13 in Group C(3), and 16 in Group D(4). There were 7 affirmative responses to the category "now separated": 2 in Group B(2), 4 in Group C(3), and 1 in Group D(4). The discrepancy of 3 between the 31 "formerly married, now single" and the 34 "now divorced" might be accounted for by annulment of marriage (not given in the responses), or possibly by an overlap of statement by those checking "now separated" who may have considered themselves "formerly married, now single." This is not clear; however, the discrepancy is *not* accounted for by those checking "widowed, now single."

Of the 34 who responded as "now cohabiting" (Table 4), the highest number, 14, were in Group B(2), the next highest, 12, in Group A(1). Group C(3) had 7, and Group D(4), 1. There may be some slight connection between the percentage of never-marrieds in Group B(2) (see Table 2), and the fact that the highest number of affirmative "now cohabiting" responses were in that age group also. The low number of total responses in the "now cohabiting" category, however, renders such a speculation suspect.

More than half of those answering the questionnaire did not elect to fill in the category concerning the number of times divorced. Of the 253 responding, 190 indicated they had never been divorced, 55 once, 6 twice, and 2 three times. Of those divorced once, 26 percent were in Group C(3) and 27 percent in Group D(4). Only one of the 17 people who responded to this question in Group A(1) had been divorced (once). Out of the 71 responding in Group B(2), 10 had been divorced once and only one person in that group had been divorced twice. Thus, as might be predicted, those who had been divorced twice or more were among the older Groups C(3) and D(4), with more time if not more inclination for marital changes.

Although only 194 out of the 525 respondents answered the query about the number of times they cohabited outside legal marriage, the elicited statistics disclosed a correlation between age and conservative practice. The percentages of *zero cohabitation* increased with age and the percentages of *cohabitation once* decreased with age. To what extent full and accurate information was given by the respondents would have to be determined by further inquiry. Table 4 contains the information for this category.

Children

Table 5 contains the information elicited concerning respondents' status relating to children. In all cases, the totals represent the number of people replying to the specific questions, not the number of people otherwise completing the questionnaire. As was to be expected, some respondents elected not to answer all questions, or overlooked answering some that might have been applicable. Also, in questions involving the number of children living or not living with respondent, there were instances where the answer was unclear as to the number of children. All of the designations in Table 5 relating to children indicate only that there was at least one child involved in each case.

Composition of Household Membership in Addition to Children

As Table 6 indicates, the numbers of relatives of spouses living in households were few compared to the numbers of friends. It is to be noted, however, that of the 40 affirmative answers to the category "friends living with you," 23 came from Group A(1) (people age 25 and under), and 14 from Group B(2) (people age 26 to 31).

The categories "legal spouse living with you" and "now legally married" were included in order to determine the relation between legal status and actual living status. The results were inconclusive. Responses are shown in Table 7.

There is a discrepancy of 68 to be noted between the number of affirmative responses to "now legally married" (323) and the total responses to "legal spouse living with you" and "now separated" (255). Since the question "now legally married" and that of "legal spouse living with you" were on separate pages in the questionnaire, some respondents may have considered it unnecessary to check "legal spouse living with you" when they came to it, considering an affirmative answer to "now legally married" sufficient to indicate cohabitation.

Religion

It will be noted from Table 8 that about 50 percent of the respondents were Protestant (40 percent of them in Group D(4)); 10 percent Catholic; 19 percent agnostic (41 percent of them in Group B(2)); 5 percent atheist; and about 5 percent Jewish. No respondents in Group D(4) claimed to be atheist.

As to strength of religious convictions (Table 9), the highest percentage, or about 32 percent, of all respondents to this question declared themselves to be "not religious" (31 percent of them in Group C(3), 30 percent in Group B(2)). Nearly as many, or about 30 percent, were "mildly religious," and about 25 percent "fairly religious." Only 14 percent stated they were "strongly religious."

Political Attitude

Considering all of the groups together, shown in Table 10, 35 percent, were politically "moderate," and 30 percent, were "liberal." The politically "conservative" comprised 23 percent and were found chiefly among the older age groups (41 percent in Group C(3), 40 percent in Group D(4)). Combining "liberal" and "moderate" categories gave a total of 65 percent of the 520 responding.

Education

Initially, all respondents were deemed to be college graduates with a B.A. or B.S. degree. From Table 11 it will be seen that many also held higher degrees. Thus, it can be inferred that the people surveyed were educationally considerably above average.

Occupation and Working Status

Job field categories as given by respondents included the following:

Business/Investments/Insurance/General contracting/Sales
Communications/Media
Community/Volunteer
Counseling/Psychology
Education
General services: Waitress/Gardener/Longshoreman/Graphic
       designer/Freelance writer/Retail clerk/Accountant/Plumber
Government: Miscellaneous Federal/State/Municipal/Civil service
Homemaker/Housewife

Law/Law enforcement
Medical arts: M.D./Dentist/Pharmacist/Physical therapist
Military services
Ministry
Scientific Research: Engineering/Biology/Biochemistry/Physics
Student

Table 12 lists job field categories given by at least 10 respondents in one or more age groups, with comparative figures.
Job description categories elicited from respondents included:

Accountant
Actuary/Insurance adjuster/Escrow officer/Insurance policy form
    drafter
Air Force/Aerospace
Army
Attorney/Public defender
Banking/Savings and loan
Broker
Clergyman
Coast Guard
Counselor/Psychologist
Crafts
Data processing/Computer marketing/Measurement systems
Dentist
Farmer/Rancher
Gardener
Homemaker
Journalist
Librarian
Manager/Director/Supervisor/Coordinator/Administrator/
    Department chairman/Owner/Partner/Executive
    secretary/Superintendent/Foreman/Ranking military officer
Navy
Negotiator/Evaluator/Programmer
Physical education coach
Practicing physician/Surgical assistant/Resident physician/Group
    practice/Medical physicist/Nurse/Dietician
College professor/College teacher
Real estate sales and development
Research fellow/Research technician
Retail store

Retired
Salesman
Secretary/Bookkeeper/Clerk/Receptionist/Court reporter/
    Administrative assistant
Sheriff/Detective/Parole officer/Patrol/Police chief/Probation
    officer/Law officer
Student/Graduate student/T.A./Ph.D. candidate
Teacher: High school or junior high school/K–3, elementary
Technician: Engineer/Chemist/Clinician
Television
Waitress

Table 13 lists job description categories given by at least 10 respondents
in one or more age groups, with comparative figures.

As shown in Table 14, more women than men were employed full time
in Group A(1), almost twice as many men as women in Group C(3), and
full-time employment figures for each sex in Groups B(2) and D(4) were
approximately equal. In all age groups there were more women working
part time than men, and more women voluntarily not working than men.
Unemployment was low and spread fairly evenly as to sex in all age
groups. It was not ascertained whether those designating themselves as
"unpaid homemakers" and those who did voluntary work also were
employed part time or were included in the "voluntarily not working"
category. There may have been overlappings in these areas.

Personal and Family Income

About 90 percent of those surveyed responded to the questions regarding income. Table 15 gives comparative figures for personal income;
Table 16 shows total family income. Almost 38 percent of the
respondents indicated that individually they earned less than $10,000 a
year; however, total family incomes under $10,000 were reported by only
15 percent of those answering. Most family incomes totaled more than
$15,000; however, only 4 percent were in the $50,000 to $99,999
category, and less than 1 percent earned $100,000 or more.

Residential Pattern

A total of three respondents lived in foreign countries. Respondents
were residents of 33 states, including Hawaii and Alaska. Residence
figures are given in Table 17.

Table 18 shows that over one-half of the respondents lived in cities of
over 50,000 population. Table 19 indicates areas of residence, whether
rural, suburban, or urban. In Table 20 there are figures for type of

residence, which disclose that 69 percent of the respondents lived in single family homes and 20 percent in apartments. Table 21, concerning status of occupancy, shows that over 61 percent of respondents owned their own homes. Figures for residential mobility are given in Table 22.

Summary of Descriptive Background of Respondents

The average age of all respondents was 35. They were 58 percent female, 42 percent male. All but 2 were U.S. citizens and 93 percent classified themselves as Anglo-American.

Seventy-seven percent of those with an average age of 23, 33 percent of those with an average age of 28, and 7 percent of those with average ages of 35 and 54 were single and never married. Only 34 people responded as being "now divorced," and 34 as "now cohabiting." Seven gave affirmative responses to the category "now separated." Of the 323 respondents answering "now legally married," 21 were in their second marriage and 6 were in their third. Only about 62 percent of respondents to the marital status question in Group B(2) gave an affirmative answer to the category "now legally married," whereas the figures for those answering affirmatively in Groups C(3) and D(4) were over 84 percent and 78 percent, respectively. More than half of those completing the questionnaire did not elect to fill in the category concerning the number of times divorced. Of the 253 responding, 190 indicated they had never been divorced, 55 once, 6 twice, and 2 three times. Although only 194 out of the 525 respondents answered the query about the number of times they cohabited outside legal marriage, the elicited figures disclosed a correlation between age and conservative practice.

As might be expected, over 92 percent of respondents under 25 years of age from Group A(1) had never had children. More significant, perhaps, was the figure of 74 percent for those in Group B(2), who ranged in age from 26 to 31. The number of respondents who had one or more children of their own living with them was 183. Ten had adoptive children living with them.

As to religion, 50 percent of the respondents were Protestant, 10 percent Catholic, 19 percent agnostic, 5 percent atheist, and about 5 percent Jewish. Only 73 respondents out of the 518 answering the query regarding religious convictions designated themselves as "strongly religious." A combined total of 280 checked the categories "mildly" and "fairly" religious. Nearly 32 percent of those responding gave an affirmative answer to the category "not religious."

Thirty-five percent of the respondents were politically "moderate" and 30 percent were "liberal." The politically "conservative" totaled 23 percent and were found chiefly among the older age groups.

There were 25 Ph.D.'s among the respondents and 107 with M.A. degrees. A total of 436 had B.A.'s and 31, B.S.'s.

Job field categories of at least 10 respondents in one or more age groups included education, housewife, sales/business/contracting, science, and student. Over 36 percent of respondents worked professionally in education.

There were at least 36 general categories of job description. Those with at least 10 respondents in one or more age groups included: college professor, manager/director, salesperson, secretary/clerk, student, and teacher. Again, the percentage of educators was high: teachers in elementary, high school, and other areas totaled over 22 percent of all respondents.

Among the youngest respondents—Group A(1)—more women than men were employed full time. In Group C(3), ages 32 through 44, almost twice as many men as women were employed full time. The totals in this category for Groups B(2) and D(4) were approximately equal as to sex. In all age groups there were more women working part time than men, and more women voluntarily not working than men. Unemployment was low and spread fairly evenly as to sex in all age groups.

Thirty-eight percent of those responding to the question regarding personal income had salaries of less than $10,000 a year. Twenty-nine percent were in the $15,000 to $24,999 bracket. Approximately 15 percent of those responding had a combined family income of less than $10,000, 33 percent earned $15,000 to $24,999, and 31 percent were in the $25,000 to $49,999 bracket. The B(2), C(3) and D(4) age groups, comprising most of those in the $15,000 to $24,999 categories, had nearly equal totals. There were 21 people in the $50,000 to $99,999 bracket, and only 2 in the $100,000-and-over category.

Although 33 states were represented, including Hawaii and Alaska, about 84 percent of all respondents lived in California. Fifty-four percent of people responding lived in cities of over 50,000 population and 41 percent lived within a city, close in, but not in the central core. Sixty-nine percent lived in single family homes and 20 percent lived in apartments. Over 61 percent owned their own homes. Groups with higher numbers of renters were in the younger age brackets, those who owned their own homes were predominantly in the higher age range.

Younger people moved more often than the older respondents. About 53 percent of the two younger age groups moved within the past year. The total for all age groups who moved within the past year was 163, or 31 percent.

FIGURE 1

(Copy of cover letter sent with Questionnaire)

Mrs. Irving F. Laucks _____

706 ROCKWOOD DRIVE   SANTA BARBARA, CALIFORNIA 93103

September 20, 1976

Dear Friend:

In connection with my work as a U.C.S.B. Ph.D. candidate, studying changes in the American family, I am making a survey of current attitudes toward children, their place in the lives of adults today, and especially their meaning for parents.

Your name has been selected as a former U.C.S.B. student, to be sent the attached questionnaire. I hope you will participate and that you will carefully fill out all the questions, adding any comments you may wish on the face of the questionnaire as you go along, or at the end in the space provided -- or on a separate sheet if necessary. I am enclosing a stamped, addressed envelope for the return of the completed form.

Your responses, of course, will be kept strictly anonymous. You need not supply your name unless you wish to be among those who will be further interviewed personally. No names or addresses will be used or linked in any way to the information finally released in aggregate form.

I appreciate your cooperation and hope to have your response soon. Thank you very much.

Very sincerely yours,

Eulah C. Laucks

Eulah C. Laucks

FIGURE 2

QUESTIONNAIRE

Please complete the following by placing a check (✓) in each appropriate
space. Where options are indicated, check (✓) appropriate option. Where
a number or other information is requested, please supply it in the appropriate space. Disregard numbers in parentheses, which are for computer use.

_____

1. AGE: ____ (1-7,8)

2. SEX: M ___ (1)   F ___ (2)   (1-9)

3. CITIZEN OF: U.S.A. ___ (1) Other (please specify) _____ (2)   (1-10)

4. ETHNIC or RACIAL IDENTITY:

    Anglo-American ___ (1)   Native Indian-American ___ (2)   Black ___ (3)   (1-11)
    Chicano ___ (4)   Asian-American ___ (5)   Other (specify) _____ (6)

5. MARITAL STATUS:

    Never Married and now Single ___ (1) (1-12) | Number of times
    Formerly Married but now Single ___ (2) | legally Married ____   (1-i6)
    Widowed and now Single ___ (3) | Number of times
    Now legally Married ___ (4) | Divorced _____   (1-17)
    Divorced ___ (1-13) | If in the past you have
    Separated from legal spouse ___ (1-14) | Cohabited, state number
                                                    | of such episodes, in-
    Now Cohabiting | cluding the present one if
    (not legally married to mate) ___ (1-15) | you are now Cohabiting ____   (1-18)

6. CHILDREN:

                    Have never had any of your own ___   (1-19)
                    Number of your own children who have died ____   (1-20)

    Number of your own children <u>living with you</u> who are:
    Under 6 years ___ (1-21)   6 or older but not yet 12 ___ (1-22)
    12 or older but not yet 18 ___ (1-23)   Over 18 years ___ (1-24)

    Number of your own children <u>not</u> living with you who are:
    Under 6 years ___ (1-25)   6 or older but not yet 12 ___ (1-26)
    12 or older but not yet 18 ___ (1-27)   Over 18 years ___ (1-28)

6. CHILDREN: (continued)

Number of stepchildren <u>living with you</u> who are:

Under 6 years ___ (1-29)   6 or older but not yet 12 ___ (1-30)

12 or older but not yet 18 ___ (1-31)   Over 18 years ___ (1-32)

Number of stepchildren <u>not</u> living with you who are:

Under 6 years ___ (1-33)   6 or older but not yet 12 ___ (1-34)

12 or older but not yet 18 ___ (1-35)   Over 18 years ___ (1-36)

Number of your adopted children <u>living with you</u> who are:

Under 6 years ___ (1-37)   6 or older but not yet 12 ___ (1-38)

12 or older but not yet 18 ___ (1-39)   Over 18 years ___ (1-40)

Number of your adopted children <u>not</u> living with you who are:

Under 6 years ___ (1-41)   6 or older but not yet 12 ___ (1-42)

12 or older but not yet 18 ___ (1-43)   Over 18 years ___ (1-44)

Number of foster children <u>living with you</u> who are:

Under 6 years ___ (1-45)   6 or older but not yet 12 ___ (1-46)

12 or older but not yet 18 ___ (1-47)   Over 18 years ___ (1-48)

Number of your common law children (born out of legal marriage) <u>living with you</u> who are

Under 6 years ___ (1-49)   6 or older but not yet 12 ___ (1-50)

12 or older but not yet 18 ___ (1-51)   Over 18 years ___ (1-52)

Number of your common law children <u>not</u> living with you who are:

Under 6 years ___ (1-53)   6 or older but not yet 12 ___ (1-54)

12 or older but not yet 18 ___ (1-55)   Over 18 years ___ (1-56)

Number of your grandchildren <u>living with you</u> under your care and responsibility who are:

Under 6 years ___ (1-57)   6 or older but not yet 12 ___ (1-58)

12 or older but not yet 18 ___ (1-59)   Over 18 years ___ (1-60)

Number of children <u>living with you</u> who are not your own and not your grandchildren, but who are related to you and under your care and responsibility, who are:

Under 6 years ___ (1-61)   6 or older but not yet 12 ___ (1-62)

12 or older but not yet 18 ___ (1-63)   Over 18 years ___ (1-64)

Number of handicapped children <u>living with you</u> who are:

Under 6 years ___ (1-65)   6 or older but not yet 12 ___ (1-66)

12 or older but not yet 18 ___ (1-67)   Over 18 years ___ (1-68)

7. Do you have any of the following living with you: (Check (✓))

    Legal Spouse ___ (1-69)   Father ___ (1-70)   Mother ___ (1-71)

    Father-in-law ___ (1-72)   Mother-in-law ___ (1-73)

    Son ___ (1-74)   Daughter ___ (1-75)

    Son-in-law ___ (1-76)   Daughter-in-law ___ (1-77)

    Other (indicate relationship: e.g. cousin, friend) _____ (1-78)

8. RELIGION: (2-7)

    Protestant ___ (1)   Catholic ___ (2)   Jewish ___ (3)

    Agnostic ___ (4)   Atheist ___ (5)   Muslim ___ (6)

    Other (please specify) _____ (7)

9. RELIGIOUS CONVICTIONS: (2-8)

    Strongly religious ___ (1)   Mildly religious ___ (2)

    Fairly religious ___ (3)   Not religious ___ (4)

10. POLITICAL ATTITUDE: (2-9)

    Radical ___ (1)   Liberal ___ (2)   Moderate ___ (3)

    Conservative ___ (4)   Very conservative ___ (5)

    Have no political attitude ___ (6) Other (specify) _____ (7)

11. EDUCATION:

    College years completed: 1 ___ (1) 2 ___ (2) 3 ___ (3) 4 ___ (4) Over 4 ___ (5) (2-10)

    Year graduated from college: 19 __ __ (2-11,12)

    Years of Graduate School completed ____ (2-13)

    Degrees: B.A. ___ (2-14) B.S. ___ (2-15) M.A. ___ (2-16) Ph.D. ___ (2-17)

        Other (specify: e.g. M.D.) _____ (2-18)

    If you have grown children, indicate highest level of schooling each has attained:

Age of Child		Sex		Ele-mentary	High School	College	Post Graduate	
		M	F					
____ (2-19,20)	___(1)	___(2)	(2-21) ___ (1)	___ (2)	___ (3)	___ (4)	(2-22)
____ (2-23,24)	___(1)	___(2)	(2-25) ___ (1)	___ (2)	___ (3)	___ (4)	(2-26)
____ (2-27,28)	___(1)	___(2)	(2-29) ___ (1)	___ (2)	___ (3)	___ (4)	(2-30)
____ (2-31,32)	___(1)	___(2)	(2-33) ___ (1)	___ (2)	___ (3)	___ (4)	(2-34)

12. OCCUPATION:

Nature of Business or Profession (e.g. Retail Selling, Obstetrics, (2-35,36)
Carpentry) _____

Title (e.g. Foreman, Supt., Pres., Self-employed) _____
                                                              (2-37)

Major duties _____ (2-38)

Does this occupation provide principal financial support of family?
                            YES ___ (1)   NO ___ (2)   (2-39)

Are earnings from this occupation auxiliary to main financial support
of family?   YES ___ (1)   NO ___ (2)   (2-40)

13. WORKING STATUS:

Full time ___ (1)   Part time ___ (2)   (2-41)

Voluntarily not working ___ (1)   (2-42)
Unemployed, unable to find remunerative work ___ (2)

Do volunteer work ___   (2-43)

Self-employed ___ (2-44)

Work as homemaker (unpaid) ___ (2-45)

14. PERSONAL INCOME: (2-46)

Under $10,000 ___ (1) $10,000 to $12,999 ___ (2)
$13,000 to $14,999 ___ (3) $15,000 to $24,999 ___ (4)
$25,000 to $49,999 ___ (5) $50,000 to $99,999 ___ (6)
                                   Over $100,000 ___ (7)

15. TOTAL FAMILY INCOME: (2-47)

Under $10,000 ___ (1) $10,000 to $12,999 ___ (2)
$13,000 to $14,999 ___ (3) $15,000 to $24,999 ___ (4)
$25,000 to $49,999 ___ (5) $50,000 to $99,999 ___ (6)
                                   $100,000 or more ___ (7)

16. RESIDENTIAL PATTERN:

Name the State in which you now reside _____ (2-48,49)

16.   RESIDENTIAL PATTERN: (continued)

Size of town or city where you live: (Check (✓))   (2-50)

Under 10,000 population ___ (1)   Over 10,000 but under 50,000 ___ (2)
Over 50,000 ___ (3)

Area of Residence: (Check (✓))   (2-51)
In rural area outside city limits ___ (1)
In suburbs within city limits ___ (2)
In a residential area close in but not in central city ___ (3)
Within central city ___ (4)

Type of Residence: (Check (✓)) (2-52)
Single family home ___ (1)
Apartment ___ (2)
Condominium ___ (3)   Rented ___ (1)   (2-53)
Duplex ___ (4)   Owned by you ___ (2)
Communal multifamily home ___ (5)

Have you moved in the last year?   YES ___ (1)   NO ___ (2)   (2-54)

Number of times you have moved in the last 4 years:
Within the same city ____ (2-55)
Outside the city where you resided 4 years ago, but within same State ____   (2-56)
Outside the city where you resided 4 years ago, and into another State
or Country ____   (2-57)

17.   ASPIRATIONS AND GOALS:
Assess the following by writing in appropriate numbers as follows:

If answer is Most Important, write 6
If answer is Highly Important, write 5
If answer is Somewhat Important, write 4
If answer is Not Very Important, write 3
If answer is Of No Importance, write 2
If answer is Have No Opinion, write 1

Making a happy life for myself ___ (2-58)
Having interesting work to do ___ (2-59)
Building myself a financially secure future ___ (2-60)
Having a satisfactory sex life ___ (2-61)

17. ASPIRATIONS AND GOALS: (continued)

Most Important	6
Highly Important	5
Somewhat Important	4
Not Very Important	3
Of No Importance	2
Have No Opinion	1

Having a happy family life ___ (2-62)

Having grandchildren in my old age ___ (2-63)

Having children to carry on the family name ___ (2-64)

Having children who will carry on my ideas and values ___ (2-65)

Providing a better future for my children ___ (2-66)

Raising children to be self-respecting citizens ___ (2-67)

Raising happy, healthy children ___ (2-68)

Raising creative children who will likely be non-conformist ___ (2-69)

Assuring my children of a college education ___ (2-70)

Continuing my own education ___ (2-71)

Having time and freedom to express and develop my own talents ___ (2-72)

Improving myself spiritually ___ (3-7)

Establishing for myself a respected place in my community ___ (3-8)

Attaining a position of influence and power ___ (3-9)

Helping make my neighborhood a decent, friendly place ___ (3-10)

Lending a hand to people in need: in my neighborhood ___ (3-11)

in my community ___ (3-12)

in the nation ___ (3-13)

in the world ___ (3-14)

Working with other people to bring brotherhood to the world ___ (3-15)

Other (please specify and indicate importance by number)

_____ (3-16)

18. ATTITUDE TOWARD THE FOLLOWING SEXUAL PRACTICES:

If you Approve and
Use or Take Part in personally, write in appropriate spaces 6

If you Disapprove but Use or Take Part in, write 5

If you Approve, but Don't Use or Take Part in, write 4

If you Disapprove, and Don't Use or Take Part in,
but Tolerate for other people, write 3

If you Don't Use or Take Part in, and Strongly Disapprove
for everyone, write .. 2

If you Have No Opinion, write 1

Premarital cohabitation ___ (3-17)

Group marriage ___ (3-18)

Homosexual cohabitation ___ (3-19)

18. ATTITUDE TOWARD THE FOLLOWING SEXUAL PRACTICES: (continued)

Use of the "Pill" ___   (3-20)

Use of the I.U.D ___   (3-21)

Use of other contraceptives
(condom, diaphragm, rhythm,etc.) ___   (3-22)

Abortion ___   (3-23)

Vasectomy ___   (3-24)

Development of a male "Pill" ___   (3-25)

Approve and Use 6
Disapprove but Use 5
Approve, Don't Use 4
Disapprove,Don't Use but Tolerate for others 3
Don't Use,Strongly Disapprove ... 2
Have No Opinion 1

INDICATE YOUR REACTIONS TO THE FOLLOWING STATEMENTS by writing in the space in front of each one the appropriate number, in accordance with the following:

If you Strongly Agree, write 5

If you Agree, But With Reservations* write 4

If you Disagree, But With Reservations* ... 3

If you Strongly Disagree, write 2

If you Have No Opinion, write 1

* In cases where you have reservations, a brief indication of their nature would be helpful.

___ 19. From my observation (or experience), the satisfactions of parenthood   (3-26)
outweigh the sacrifices and heartaches involved.

___ 20. Childless married couples are usually frustrated and unhappy.   (3-27)

___ 21. Children are the chief source of meaning and purpose in life.   (3-28)

___ 22. The coming of children improves marital relationships.   (3-29)

___ 23. A child is part of a divine plan -- perhaps a unique creation of   (3-30)
Divine Providence.

___ 24. Producing a child proves that a person is sexually mature.   (3-31)

___ 25. People should leave to chance -- or Providence -- the having or   (3-32)
not having of children.

___ 26. Every married couple should have the right to choose whether or not   (3-33)
to have children, and the number.

___ 27. Parents should have primary responsibility for the care, support,   (3-34)
protection and entertainment of their children.

___ 28. The federal government, or perhaps the United Nations, should now   (3-35)
decide how many children each person should procreate.

___ 29. People who are on welfare should be denied the right to procreate   (3-36)
while being supported by public funds.

___ 30. Raising children today would be easier if there were some official   (3-37)
governmental standards for acceptable family comportment, so that
parents would have guidelines to measure against.

___ 31. Public government-sponsored child care centers would constitute   (3-38)

invasion of the parental right to rear children according to
individual family preference.

Strongly Agree	5
Agree, With Reservations ..	4
Disagree, With Reservations	3
Strongly Disagree	2
Have No Opinion	1

REACTIONS TO STATEMENTS:(continued from Page 7)

____ 32. Public schools today constitute a threat to parents' rights and   (3-39)
individual family values.

____ 33. Family decisions should be arrived at democratically, with each member,   (3-40)
including children as young as 4 years, having equal vote.

____ 34. Family decisions should be arrived at by equal vote of only those   (3-41)
members who are over 12 years of age.

____ 35. Both parents, sharing equally, should make all decisions concerning such   (3-42)
matters as family life style, money, job selection, home location,
choice of schools, etc.

____ 36. If parents can't come to agreement on family decisions, the father   (3-43)
should have the final word.

____ 37. In serious parental disagreements over training and discipline of   (3-44)
children, the father's method should finally prevail.

____ 38. In serious parental disagreements involving training and discipline of   (3-45)
children, the mother's way should prevail, since she usually has the
basic job of training the children.

____ 39. If parents often can't agree regarding basic methods of training and   (3-46)
discipline of children, they should call in outside counsel as soon
as possible.

____ 40. It has been said that lowering the legal age status to 18 years may be a   (3-47)
step in the direction of liberating parents from responsibility for
children who have grown unmanageable but not sufficiently delinquent to
be made wards of a court. There ought to be available some kind of
socially acceptable legal "divorce" for parents from such children, just
as there is from incompatible spouses.

____ 41. The nuclear family, consisting only of father, mother and children, is   (3-48)
no longer a good environment in which to raise children.

____ 42. People should try to live closer to their kinfolk so that blood-related   (3-49)
extended families could again become the prevalent family pattern.

____ 43. Some kind of contemporary extended family should be devised that would   (3-50)
include non-blood related people, but would not be exclusive (as are
some contemporary "communes"), but would countenance including
strangers who happened to be neighbors in the vicinity.

____ 44. Intentional extended families without patriarchs can be made to work.   (3-51)

<u>RECORD</u> <u>YOUR</u> <u>REACTIONS</u> <u>TO</u> <u>THE</u> <u>FOLLOWING</u> by writing numbers in the appropriate
spaces, in accordance with the following:

> If you feel the answer is <u>Indispensable</u>, write .. 6
>
> If the answer is <u>Very</u> <u>Valuable</u>, write 5
>
> If the answer is <u>Somewhat</u> <u>Valuable</u>, write 4
>
> If the answer is <u>Not</u> <u>Very</u> <u>Valuable</u>, write 3
>
> If the answer is <u>Of</u> <u>No</u> <u>Value</u>, write 2
>
> If you <u>Have</u> <u>No</u> <u>Opinion</u>, write 1

___ 45. The following attributes are valuable for a child to develop in order to
have a satisfactory life in today's world:

Self-sufficiency ___ (3-52)   Toughness ___ (3-58)   Adaptability ___ (3-64)

Competitiveness ___ (3-53)   Impassiveness ___ (3-59) Consistency ___ (3-65)

Tolerance ___ (3-54)   Gentleness ___ (3-60)   Assertiveness ___ (3-66)

Sociability ___ (3-55)   Cooperation ___ (3-61)   Candor ___ (3-67)

Loyalty ___ (3-56)   Perseverance ___ (3-62)   Good self image ___ (3-68)

Detachment ___ (3-57)   Shrewdness ___ (3-63)   Compassion ___ (3-69)

Other (specify and indicate value by number) _____ (3-70)

<u>RECORD</u> <u>YOUR</u> <u>ATTITUDE</u> <u>TOWARD</u> <u>THE</u> <u>FOLLOWING</u> <u>RULES</u> <u>FOR</u> <u>REARING</u> <u>CHILDREN</u> by writing
in the space in front of each one the appropriate number, as follows:

> If you <u>Strongly</u> <u>Agree</u>, write 5
>
> If you <u>Agree</u> <u>With</u> <u>Reservations</u>*, write ... 4
>
> If you <u>Disagree</u> <u>With</u> <u>Reservations</u>*, write 3
>
> If you <u>Strongly</u> <u>Disagree</u>, write 2
>
> If you <u>Have</u> <u>No</u> <u>Opinion</u>, write 1
>
> *In cases where you have reservations, a brief
> indication of their nature would be helpful.

___ 46. Punishment of children should not be severe but it should be swift   (3-71)
and certain.

___ 47. More time should be spent praising good behavior than showing disapproval   (3-72)
of bad behavior.

___ 48. Children's infractions should be discussed at length with them from the   (3-73)
time they are toddlers.

___ 49. Changing rules is confusing to children. Rules made that are reasonable   (3-74)
should not be changed, even though parents may have second thoughts
about their fairness or usefulness.

___ 50. Rules should be as few as possible and fully explained, but reasons for   (3-75)
making them should not be given.

Strongly Agree	5
Agree, With Reservations ..	4
Disagree, With Reservations	3
Strongly Disagree	2
Have No Opinion	1

ATTITUDE TOWARD RULES FOR REARING CHILDREN: (continued)

___ 51. Parental honesty is crucial. Hypocrisy cannot be hidden from children.   (4-7)

___ 52. Lecturing or warning children is a waste of breath.   (4-8)

___ 53. As children reach sub-teenage, some rules may be subject to compromise,   (4-9)
but those which are really important to parents, and are expressive of
their basic values, should not be compromised but strictly enforced, no
matter what other parents may be doing to the contrary.

___ 54. From early age, children should be constantly encouraged to assume re-   (4-10)
sponsibility for their decisions, and, as they show capacity to do so,
they should be allowed to make important decisions for themselves.

___ 55. As long as a child does not indulge in destructive behavior, he should be   (4-11)
allowed and encouraged to follow his own inclinations, even though this
may result in development of tendencies and interests not preferred for
him by his parents.

___ 56. Children should not be expected to show more self control than parents do.   (4-12)

___ 57. What is most important to children's self-image is what they think their   (4-13)
parents think of them.

___ 58. What is most important to teenage children's self-image is what they   (4-14)
think their peers think of them.

IF YOU ARE A PARENT, please also answer the following by checking (✓) appropriate spaces:

59. Please specify which of the following best describes why you became a parent   (4-15)
the first time: (Check (✓))

It happened accidentally ___ (1)

I thought that's what was expected in marriage ___ (2)

I wanted something of my very own to take care of and have the say about ___ (3)

I wanted to give someone else the happy childhood I never had ___ (4)

I felt my marriage would be more complete with a child ___ (5)

I wanted to please my mate ___ (6)

I thought a child would save my faltering marriage ___ (7)

Because of religious convictions ___ (8)

Other (please specify) _____ (9)

IF YOU ARE A PARENT: (continued)

60. If you are a parent of more than one child, please designate which of the
     following <u>best</u> describes why you had your second child (subsequent children)
     by writing appropriate number of reason in each space following child number:

    (1) It happened accidentally.

    (2) I thought that's what was expected
        in marriage.

    (3) I wanted my child (children) to have
        brother(s), sister(s).

    (4) I wanted to give more than one child   2nd Child ____   (4-16)
        the happy childhood I never had.

    (5) I felt my marriage would be more com-   3rd Child ____   (4-17)
        plete with an expanded family.

    (6) I wanted to please my mate.   4th Child
                                                       (or more) ____   (4-18)
    (7) I thought another child would save
        my faltering marriage.

    (8) I thought another child would keep
        me young.

    (9) Because of religious convictions.

  (10) Other (please specify) _____

       _____

61. There has been some discussion in the media lately indicating that a   (4-19)
     substantial percentage of parents would not have had children if they had
     it to do over again. How do you feel about this? (Check (✓))

    If I had it to do over again: I would not have any children ___ (1)

                            I would have only one child ___ (2)

                            I would have only two children ___ (3)

                            I'd have the number I do have ___ (4)

                            I'd have as many as came ___ (5)

                            I am undecided ___ (6)

62. How much time per day do (did) you spend playing or conversing with   (4-20)
     your child (children)? (Check (✓))

    Less than half an hour ___ (1) One hour ___ (2) More than one hour ___ (3)

63. If you use (used) babysitters, please check (✓) type used most often: (4-21)

    Grandparents ___ (1)   Other relatives ___ (2)   Friends ___ (3)

    Paid outsiders, in your home ___ (4)   Paid outsiders, in their home ___ (5)

    Day care centers ___ (6)   Other (specify) _____ (7)

IF YOU ARE A PARENT: (continued)

64. How long per day is (was) television the babysitter? (Check (✓))   (4-22)

    Less than 1 hour ___ (1)   1 hour ___ (2)   2 hours ___ (3)

    3 hours ___ (4)   4 hours or more ___ (5)

65. If you have (or had while parenting) paid household help (other than   (4-23,24)

    babysitters) state: Number of hours per week _____

66. When living with you, does (did) your child (children) under 15 years   (4-25)
    regularly eat dinner with you?   YES ___ (1)   NO ___ (2)

67. When living with you, does (did) your child (children) under 15 years   (4-26)
    have regular, specific chores to do?   YES ___ (1)   NO ___ (2)

68. If any of the following deters (deterred) you from having a first child,
    or subsequent children, please indicate which of the reasons best
    describes each case, by writing appropriate number in each space
    following the child number:

    (1) Possibility of nuclear war.

    (2) Unstable global economic conditions.   1st Child ____   (4-27)

    (3) Unstable national economic conditions.

    (4) Possibility of conventional wars that   2nd Child ____   (4-28)
         may involve the U.S.

    (5) High cost of raising children.   3rd Child ____   (4-29)

    (6) Disinclination to add to an
         overpopulated world.   4th Child
                                       (or more) ____   (4-30)

    (7) Belief that the world now is not a fit
         place in which to raise children.

    (8) Other (specify) _____

69. What percentage of disagreements between spouses, cohabitants or other   (4-31)
    adults in your home, concern (concerned) children of the household? (Check (✓))
    Zero% ___ (1)   10% ___ (2)   20% ___ (3)   50% ___ (4)   Over 50% ___ (5)

70. What specifically causes (caused) disagreements, concerning children, between
    spouses, cohabitants or other adults, in your home? (Check (✓))

    Differences regarding child's (children's) behavioral training ___ (4-32)

    Differences regarding child's (children's) religious training ___ (4-33)

    Differences as to methods of correction ___ (4-34)

    Differences as to which adult should have final say about punishment ___ (4-35)

    Differences about behavior of stepchildren ___ (4-36)

    School troubles ___ (4-37)   Troubles with neighbors ___ (4-38)

    Feelings of incapacity to cope with recalcitrant children ___ (4-39)

    Money difficulties involving costs of raising children ___ (4-40)

    Other (specify) _____ (4-41)

IF YOU ARE A PARENT: (continued)

71. In the parental task of raising children: (Check (✓))

    Do (did) you find schools:
    Supportive of your values ___ (1) Contradictory ___ (2) Indifferent ___ (3)   (4-42)

    Do (did) you find church influence:
    Supportive of your values ___ (1) Contradictory ___ (2) Indifferent ___ (3)   (4-43)

    What other community institutions or people do (did) you find supportive?   (4-44)
    (please specify)_____

Please answer the following by writing the appropriate number in the space in front
of each question, in accordance with the following:

                 If the answer is Very Definitely, write 6
                 If the answer is To A High Degree, write 5
                 If the answer is To A Moderate Degree, write 4
                 If the answer is To A Small Degree, write ... 3
                 If the answer is Not At All, write 2
                 If you Have No Opinion, write 1

___ 72. If you are divorced, do you feel your own offspring/step-offspring/   (4-45)
      adopted offspring (circle which) was (were) a basic source of the
      conflict that led up to the divorce?

___ 73. If divorced, do you think you would have had the divorce if there   (4-46)
      were no children in your family?

___ 74. If you are now married, or separated, and have had thoughts of divorcing,   (4-47)
      does a child (children) stand in the way of your getting the divorce?

___ 75. Does (did) it comfort you to talk to someone about the troubles you have   (4-48)
      (had) with your offspring?

___ 76. Do (did) you take satisfaction in having (an) obedient child (children)?   (4-49)

___ 77. Do you take personal satisfaction in being told your child (children)   (4-50)
      is (are) attractive, talented or well-mannered?

___ 78. Does it give you pleasure to be known as someone's mother or father?   (4-51)

___ 79. Do you feel personally triumphant in your offspring's accomplishments?   (4-52)

___ 80. Do you think of your child (children) as (an) interesting project(s)   (4-53)
      to direct?

___ 81. Do you feel that successful children add to one's status in the community,   (4-54)
      or among friends?

___ 82. Do you feel you would be missing something important to your personal   (4-55)
      development if you didn't have at least one child?

___ 83. Do you believe people should sacrifice for their children?   (4-56)

IF YOU ARE A <u>PARENT</u>: (continued)

| Very Definitely ....6 |
| To a High Degree ...5 |
| To a Moderate Degree4 |
| To a Small Degree ..3 |
| Not at All ....2 |
| Have No Opinion ....1 |

84. Is (was) your child (children) a <u>hindrance</u> to you in any of
the following pursuits: (Use key opposite for rating degree)

    Job selection ___   (4-57)

    Travel opportunities ___   (4-58)

    General mobility ___   (4-59)

    Saving money ___   (4-60)

    Staying out of debt ___   (4-61)

    Having free time for personal pursuits ___   (4-62)

    Other (please specify) _____ (4-63)

85. **When** your child (children) is (was) grossly disobedient, do (did) you
take it as: (Use above key for rating degree)

    An affront to your right as a parent ___   (4-64)

    A sign of your failure as a parent ___   (4-65)

    Other (specify and rate) _____ (4-66)

86. Do you expect your child (children) to remain close to you when you are old?   (4-67)

                                       YES ___ (1)   NO ___ (2)

87. Do you depend on their taking care of you when you are old?   (4-68)

                                       YES ___ (1)   NO ___ (2)

IF YOU ARE A <u>FEMALE</u> PARENT, please answer <u>also</u> the following, using the same key
(shown at the top of this page) for rating degree:

___ 88. Is (was) your desire to have a child (children) prompted by wanting   (4-69)
"something to do"?

___ 89. Was pregnancy your "finest hour"?   (4-70)

___ 90. Do (did) you feel that emotionally you <u>need</u> (needed) to be pregnant   (4-71)
every so often?

___ 91. Do you think there is a basic female need to experience having and   (4-72)
rearing children?

___ 92. Did you enjoy the attention being pregnant afforded?   (4-73)

___ 93. Did you become pregnant to please your parents?   (4-74)

___ 94. Did you become pregnant to please your mate?   (4-75)

IF YOU ARE WILLING TO BE INTERVIEWED FURTHER IN PERSON, PLEASE GIVE:

                        Your Name: _____

                        Address: _____

                                    _____

                        Phone Number _____

COMMENTS: _____

TABLE 1: AGE, SEX, CITIZENSHIP, ETHNICITY

	A (1)	B (2)	C (3)	D (4)	Totals
Average age of respondents:	23.35	27.92	35.03	53.77	35.02
Sex:	M / F 39 56	M / F 63 76	M / F 65 87	M / F 55 84	M / F 222 303=525
Citizenship:	US/other 93 2	US/other 139	US/other 152	US/other 139	US/other 523 2
Ethnicity: (AA=Anglo-American) No response B(2)/Male	AA/other 84 11	AA/other 127 10 (2)	AA/other 142 10	AA/other 131 8	AA/other 484 39=523 2

TABLE 2: MARITAL STATUS

	A(1)	B(2)	C(3)	D(4)	Totals
Never Married, Single	70	43	10	10	133
Formerly Married, Single	2	6	9	12	29
Widowed/Now Single			1	6	7
Now Legally Married	19	82	119	103	323 494
No Response	4	8	13	8	31 525

TABLE 3: NUMBER OF TIMES LEGALLY MARRIED

Distribution of the 361 responses to the question involving the number of times legally married was as follows:

	A(1)	B(2)	C(3)	D(4)	Totals
Zero	11	15	1	4	31
Once	15	78	111	96	300
Twice		4	10	10	24*
Three times			2	4	6
No response	69	42	28	25	361 164 525

*There is no discrepancy between this total of 24 and the text reference to 21 respondents who were in their second legal marriage. Three of the 24 above did not classify themselves as being "Now Legally Married"; 2 in Group B(2) and 1 in Group C(3). They could have been married twice without currently being legally married.

TABLE 4: NUMBER OF TIMES COHABITED

	A(1)	B(2)	C(3)	D(4)	Totals
Zero	6	23	26	24	79
Once	17	42	17	4	80
Twice	3	13	2	3	21
Three times		5	4	2	11
Four times		1	1		2
9 Times or More				1	1
No response					194 331 525
Respondents Now Cohabiting	12	14	7	1	34

TABLE 5:   CHILDREN

	A(1)	B(2)	C(3)	D(4)	Totals
Never had own children	88	103	34	18	243
Had one child who died			5	8	13
Had two who died			1	2	3
Had three who died				1	1
Own child under 6, living with you	1	20	44		65
Own child over 6, under 12, living with you		5	34	2	41'
Own child over 12, under 18, living with you			14	22	36*
Own child, over 18, living with you				41	41
Own child, under 6, not living with you			3		3
Own child, over 6. under 12, not living with you		1	1		2
Own child, over 12. under 18, not living with you		1	3	1	5
Own child, over 18, not living with you			1	30	31
Stepchild, under 6 not living with you		1			1
Stepchild, over 12 but under 18, not living with you			1		1

TABLE 5 (continued)

	A(1)	B (2)	C(3)	D(4)	Totals
Stepchild, over 18, <u>not</u> living with you				2	2
Adopted child, under 6, living with you			3		3
Adopted child, over 6, but under 12, living with you			4	1	5
Adopted child, over 12, but under 18, living with you				2	2
Adopted child, over 6, but under 12, <u>not</u> living with you				1	1
Adopted child, over 12, but under 18, <u>not</u> living with you			1	1	2
Adopted child, over 18, <u>not</u> living with you				3	3
Common Law child, over 12, but under 18, <u>not</u> living with you			1		1
Common Law child, over 18, <u>not</u> living with you				2	2
Grandchild, over 6, but under 12, living with you				1	1
Grandchild, over 12, but under 18, living with you				1	1
Grandchild, over 18 living with you				1	1
Handicapped child, over 18, living with you			1		1

TABLE 6: COMPOSITION OF HOUSEHOLD MEMBERSHIP IN ADDITION TO CHILDREN

	A(1)	B(2)	C(3)	D(4)	Totals
Father living with you	12	4	1	3	20
Mother living with you	17	5	2	3	27
Father-in-law living with you			1		1
Mother-in-law living with you		1		4	5
One or more sons living with you		15	55	28	98
One or more daughters living with you	1	7	53	26	87
Daughter-in-law living with you				1	1
Friends living with you	23	14	3		40
Bro-in-law/Sis-in-law living with you		2			2
Brother/Sister living with you	4	2			6
Niece/Nephew living with you			1		1
Grandfather/Grandmother living with you	1				1
Cousin living with you	1				1

TABLE 7: LEGAL MARITAL STATUS/ACTUAL LIVING STATUS

	A(1)	B(2)	C(3)	D(4)	Totals
Now Legally Married	19	82	119	103	323
Legal Spouse Living With You	15	62	99	72	248
Now Separated		2	4	1	7

TABLE 8: RELIGION

	A(1)	B(2)	C(3)	D(4)	Totals
Protestant	26	46	80	102	254
Catholic	12	13	17	11	53
Jewish	12	8	2	1	23
Agnostic	25	40	23	10	98
Atheist	6	7	15		28
Other	11	24	13	12	60
					516
No Response	3	1	2	3	9
					525

TABLE 9: RELIGIOUS CONVICTIONS

	A(1)	B(2)	C(3)	D(4)	Totals
Strongly religious	6	17	22	28	73
Mildly religious	27	42	38	46	153
Fairly religious	18	28	38	43	127
Not religious	43	50	51	21	165
					518
No Response	1	2	3	1	7
					525

TABLE 10:   POLITICAL ATTITUDE

	A(1)	B(2)	C(3)	D(4)	Totals
Radical	5	1	4	1	11
Liberal	50	53	30	23	156
Moderate	24	46	57	57	184
Conservative	4	18	49	48	119
Very conservative	1	2	2	3	8
No political attitude	3	9	4		16
Other, unspecified	6	9	5	6	26
					520
No Response	2	1	1	1	5
					525

TABLE 11:   EDUCATION

	A(1)	B(2)	C(3)	D(4)	Totals
B.A.	94	110	127	105	436
B.S.	1	10	12	8	31
One year of graduate school	33		22	31	86
Two years graduate school	3		29	22	54
Elementary or secondary teaching credential	4	22	8	3	37
M.A.	5	20	45	37	107
Ph.D.		8	16	1	25

TABLE 12: JOB FIELD CATEGORIES WITH
AT LEAST 10 RESPONDENTS IN ONE OR MORE AGE GROUPS ·

	A(1)	B(2)	C(3)	D(4)	Totals
Education	11	40	64	77	192
Housewife		7	14	7	28
Sales/Business/ Contracting	24	29	27	18	98
Science	2	8	11	1	22
Student	22	12	2		36
No field	5	2	8	13	28

TABLE 13. JOB DESCRIPTION CATEGORIES WITH
AT LEAST 10 RESPONDENTS IN ONE OR MORE AGE GROUPS ·

	A(1)	B(2)	C(3)	D(4)	Totals
College professor		3	12	1	16
Manager/Director	7	16	16	26	65
Salesperson (including Real Estate)	8	3	5	4	20
Secretary/Clerk	17	9	8	4	38
Self-employed	6	6	12	7	31
Student	15	10			25
Teacher (including elementary High school, undesig- nated)	7	26	38	48	119

TABLE 14: WORKING STATUS

	A(1)		B(2)		C(3)		D(4)		Totals		Combined Total
	M	F	M	F	M	F	M	F	M	F	
Employed full time	18	30	51	52	61	33	46	49	176	164	= 340
Employed part time	10	16	6	13	1	26	1	14	18	69	= 87
Unemployed, unable to find renumerative work	3	3	2	2		4		1	5	10	= 15
Voluntarily not working	5	9	3	4	3	15	3	11	14	39	= 53
Do Voluntary work	2	2	3	3	2	20		17	7	42	= 49
Unpaid Homemaker		1		12	1	41	1	27	2	81	= 83

TABLE 15: PERSONAL INCOME

	A(1)	B(2)	C(3)	D(4)	Totals
Under $10,000	71	51	35	22	179
$10,000 to $12,999	13	26	8	5	52
$13,000 to 14,999	3	18	17	12	50
$15,000 to $24,999	3	35	46	54	138
$25,000 to $49,999	1	4	18	26	49
$50,000 to $99,999			4	1	5
$100,000 and over	None	None	None	None	
Total Responses					473

TABLE 16: TOTAL FAMILY INCOME

	A(1)	B(2)	C(3)	D(4)	Totals
Under $10,000	44	24	2	2	72
$10,000 to $12,999	9	15	8	2	34
$13,000 to $14,999	4	13	14	15	46
$15,000 to $24,999	7	55	57	41	160
$25,000 to $49,999	11	22	60	59	152
$50,000 to $99,999	2	4	8	7	21
$100,000 and over		1		1	2
Total responses					487

TABLE 17: RESIDENCE BY STATES

	A(1)	B(2)	C(3)	D(4)	Totals
California	81	116	113	124	434
Other	12	21	39	12	84 / 518
No response					7 / 525

TABLE 18: SIZE OF TOWN OR CITY OF RESIDENCE

	A(1)	B(2)	C(3)	D(4)	Totals
Under 10,000	12	24	16	18	70
Over 10,000, Under 50,000	22	45	52	42	161
Over 50,000	60	67	80	74	281
No Response	1	3	4	5	13 / 525

TABLE 19:   AREA OF RESIDENCE

	A(1)	B(2)	C(3)	D(4)	Totals
Rural, outside city limits	7	28	26	35	96
Suburbs, within city limits	31	52	47	43	173
Within city, close in but not central	43	47	71	52	213
Within central city	14	12	5	7	38
No Response			3	2	5
					525

TABLE 20:   TYPE OF RESIDENCE

	A(1)	B(2)	C(3)	D(4)	Totals
Single family home	37	74	131	120	362
Apartment	45	39	12	10	106
Condominium	5	10	2	4	21
Duplex	5	13	4	4	26
Communal/Multi-family	3	3	1	1	8
No Response					2
					525

TABLE 21 :   STATUS OF OCCUPANCY

	A(1)	B(2)	C(3)	D(4)	Totals
Rented home	67	68	26	5	166
Owned home	11	50	97	108	266
No Response	17	21	29	26	93
					525

TABLE 22 :   RESIDENTIAL MOBILITY

	A(1)	B(2)	C(3)	D(4)	Totals
Moved in the last year	64	59	31	9	163

5

Attitudes and Opinions
of Respondents

The second part of the questionnaire was devised to elicit attitudes, opinions, and statements that might illuminate the posture of respondents toward children, as well as respondents' notions with respect to the meaning of children in contemporary society.

Descriptive Note on Tables 23 Through 55

Tables 23, 24, 25, and 26 set forth responses of Groups A(1), B(2), C(3), and D(4) to twenty-five statements relating to their aspirations and goals. Table 27 contains comparative responses of Groups A(1), B(2), C(3), and D(4) to four categories of aspirations and goals: those chiefly self-serving; those serving family; those directed toward the welfare of children; and those serving social aims of the community, nation, or world. Table 28 gives information relating to respondents' attitudes toward sexual practices. Table 29 sets forth respondents' attitudes toward the need, desirability, and responsibility of parenthood. Some of the statements in this section of the questionnaire were intentionally devised to be provocative. Attitudes concerning family decisions and disagreements will be found in Table 30. Tables 31, 32, 33, and 34 set forth attitudes toward rules for rearing children for each age group of respondents.

Tables 35, 36, 37, and 38, show each group's choices of attributes thought to be valuable or not valuable for a child to develop in order to have a satisfactory life in today's world. Table 39 is a comparison of all groups' choices of child attributes considered most valuable or indispensable. The "most valuable" and "indispensable" categories were combined to represent a high affirmation block of the continuum and thus to arrive at a list of most desired attributes or characteristics. The comparisons are in percentages. Table 40 compares two factors important to children's self-images: (1) what they think their parents think of them, and (2) what they think their peers think of them.

Table 41 gives parental reasons for having had a first child, and Table

42 gives parental reasons for having had a second and/or subsequent children. Table 43 sets forth reasons deterring respondents from having a first and/or subsequent children. Parental opinions regarding children as a hindrance to personal pursuits are found in Table 44.

Table 45 indicates percentages of disagreements among adults in the home that concerned children. Causes of these disagreements over children are given in Table 46. Attitudes toward the influence of children on divorce decisions are shown in Table 47.

Table 48 contains some factors meant to elicit the degree of parental attentiveness shown by respondents. The intention of the questions in Table 49, dealing with some of the more subjective feelings and attitudes toward parenthood, was to elicit what reflective importance children may have for parents. Table 50 resulted from asking the question made famous by Ann Landers' column: If you had it to do over again, would you become a parent, and if so, how many children would you choose to have? The purpose of the questions in Table 51 was to elicit the degree of respondents' intention to be dependent on their children in later life. Questions in Table 52 were addressed exclusively to female parents in an attempt to uncover any distinctly female reactions to childbearing.

Attitudes of respondents toward the influence of government, schools, and churches on procreation and child rearing are found in Table 53. Table 54 contains parental evaluations of the support afforded them by schools, churches, and other community institutions in the process of child rearing. Table 55 sets forth attitudes of respondents relating to the nuclear family and the extended family.

Some Observations on the Tables

Aspirations and Goals

The following observations may be noted from Table 27, in which, for comparative study, the responses in Tables 23, 24, 25, and 26 are put into the four age categories. About 80 to 90 percent of respondents in all groups found making a happy life for themselves and having interesting work to do highly important. Around 50 percent rated as highly important building a financially secure future for themselves and having a satisfactory sex life.

Having grandchildren in old age or having children to carry on personal ideas and values were deemed not very important by well over half of all respondents except those in Group D(4), the oldest group, 40 percent of which rated these categories "of no importance/not very important."

Sixty-eight percent of the youngest respondents and 43 percent of the group 26 through 31 years of age rated continuing their own education highly important. Less than a third of the two older groups found this an important goal.

All respondents rated having time and freedom to express and develop personal talents very highly. Forty percent or fewer of all respondents aspired to improve themselves spiritually. The highest percentage (40.1) was found in Group D(4). In general, establishing a respected place in the community and attaining a position of influence and power were deemed unimportant.

All respondents emphasized the importance of having a happy family life, but considered as not very important having children to carry on the family name. Around 50 percent of all respondents were interested in providing a better future for their children, and over 75 percent cited the goal of raising happy, healthy children. Less than 50 percent of respondents rated assuring their children a college education as highly important.

Aspirations and goals serving social aims were mixed. Over 52 percent of all respondents rated raising children to be good citizens as highly important. (In fact, an overwhelming 90 percent of respondents in Group D(4) considered this highly important.) However, only respondents in Group A(1) showed strong interest (34 percent) in raising nonconformist children.

All respondents placed more emphasis on community and neighborhood goals than on those of the nation or the world. Personal and immediate family goals carried more weight than broader social aims.

Attitudes Toward Sexual Practices

The following observations are derived from data presented in Table 28.

Slightly more than 8 percent of all respondents strongly disapproved of premarital cohabitation for everyone; 23 percent disapproved but tolerated it for others; 34 percent approved but did not take part in it; and 32 percent approved and themselves practiced it. The highest number of respondents strongly disapproving of premarital cohabitation for everyone were in Group D(4). Twenty-one percent of them were strongly opposed. The highest number of those disapproving of cohabitation but tolerating the practice for others was also found in the oldest group of respondents — over 41 percent of them answered that query affirmatively. About half of Groups A(1) and B(2), 20 percent of Group C(3), and 12 percent of Group D(4) approved of and took part in premarital cohabitation.

Over 32 percent of all respondents strongly disapproved of group marriage for everyone; 51 percent of these were in Group D(4). Over 37 percent of all respondents indicated tolerance of group marriage for others. Eighty-two percent of all those approving of group marriage but not themselves practicing it were in the two younger groups. There was only one person, in Group C(3), who approved of and was taking part in group marriage.

Twenty-one percent of all respondents strongly disapproved of homosexual cohabitation. Eighty percent of them were in Groups C(3) and D(4). Of those disapproving of but tolerating homosexual cohabitation in other people (34 percent of all respondents), 62 percent were found in Groups C(3) and D(4). Most of those approving of but not practicing homosexual cohabitation were found in Groups A(1) and B(2). They represented two-thirds of the 37 percent replying affirmatively to this question. Less than 2 percent (8 people) in all groups stated they approved of and took part in homosexual cohabitation.

Only 4 percent of the respondents strongly disapproved of the use of the birth control pill, half of them in Group D(4). Only 9 percent of the total respondents disapproved of its use but tolerated it for other people. Over 51 percent of all respondents approved of the birth control pill but did not use it themselves. Over 60 percent of this number were in Groups C(3) and D(4). Those who approved of and used the pill totaled 30 percent of all respondents, 68 percent of whom were in Groups B(2) and C(3). About 35 percent of Group A(1) respondents approved of and used the birth control pill, 42 percent of Group B(2), 31 percent of Group C(3), and 13 percent of Group D(4).

Only 5 percent of the respondents, half of whom were in Group D(4), strongly disapproved of the use of the I.U.D. (intra-uterine device) for birth control for everyone. Eight percent, one-third of whom were in Group D(4), disapproved but tolerated its use for others. Sixty-seven percent of all respondents approved of but did not use the I.U.D.: 76 percent of Group A(1), 69 percent of Group B(2), 67 percent of Group C(3), and 61 percent of Group D(4). Only 13 percent, mostly in Groups B(2) and C(3), approved of and used the I.U.D.

Approximately 58 percent of all respondents approved of but did not use other contraceptives (condom, diaphragm, rhythm, etc.). This percentage was distributed fairly equally among all groups. About a third of all respondents approved of and used other contraceptives. Affirmative responses to this query were also fairly evenly divided among all groups.

Only 8 percent of the respondents strongly disapproved of abortion, and 15 percent tolerated it for others. Sixty-one percent of all respondents approved of abortion but did not themselves use it, and 13 percent approved of and had used abortion: 16 percent of Group A(1), 16 percent of Group B(2), 12 percent of Group C(3), and 8 percent of Group D(4).

Less than 2 percent of the respondents strongly disapproved of vasectomy and 4 percent disapproved but tolerated it for others. Over 75 percent of all respondents approved of but did not themselves use vasectomy: 22 percent were in Group A(1), 31 percent in Group B(2), 27 percent in Group C(3), and 21 percent in Group D(4). Those who approved of and had used vasectomy were 17 percent of total respondents. Approximately 39 percent of these were in Group C(3) and 42 percent in Group D(4).

Only 3 percent of the respondents stated that they strongly disapproved of the development of a male birth control pill, and 3 percent said they disapproved but would tolerate it for others. Seventy percent of all respondents were in favor of the development, although they would not use a male birth control pill themselves; 13 percent stated they would both approve of development for such a pill and use it. Affirmative answers to these two queries were fairly evenly distributed across all age groups.

Attitudes Toward Need, Desirability, and Responsibility of Parenthood

This section contains information that may be noted from Table 29 concerning attitudes toward need, desirability, and responsibility of parenthood.

With respect to whether satisfactions outweigh sacrifices of parenthood, 35 percent of those responding in Group A(1) strongly agreed, and about 40 percent agreed with reservations; 35 percent of Group B(2) strongly agreed, and about 44 percent agreed with reservations; 57 percent of those responding in Group C(3) strongly agreed, and 32 percent agreed with reservations; and 69 percent of Group D(4) strongly agreed, and 23 percent agreed with reservations. Thus, over half of all respondents strongly agreed that the satisfactions of parenthood outweigh the sacrifices and heartaches involved, and 34 percent agreed with reservations.

At least 52 percent of all respondents strongly disagreed with the statement that childless married couples are usually frustrated and unhappy, and another 25 percent disagreed with reservations. The group that strongly disagreed was composed of 63 percent of Group A(1), 63 percent of Group B(2), 56 percent of Group C(3), and only 31 percent of Group D(4). Only 12 people out of the 522 responding (2 percent) strongly agreed with the premise.

Forty-six percent of the respondents strongly disagreed with the statement that children are the chief source of meaning and purpose in life. Twenty-five percent disagreed with reservations. Approximately 20 percent agreed with reservations and only 7 percent strongly agreed. Of those strongly disagreeing, Group A(1) respondents made up 27 percent, Group B(2) 35 percent, Group C(3) 26 percent, and Group D(4) only 12 percent.

Again, a higher percentage in Group D(4) than in the other groups agreed that the coming of children improves marital relationships, with 32 percent of Group D(4) respondents strongly agreeing or agreeing with reservations. Of all respondents who strongly disagreed (40.6 percent of total respondents), 20 percent were in Group A(1), 33 percent in Group B(2), 29 percent in Group C(3), and only 18 percent in Group D(4).

Those strongly disagreeing that a child is a part of a divine plan — perhaps a unique creation of Divine Providence — numbered 237 out of 520, or 46 percent. This was 54 percent of Groups A(1) and B(2), 48 percent of Group C(3) and only 28 percent of Group D(4). Thus, respondents age 45 and over were least in disagreement with the statement. In fact, 24 percent of Group D(4) strongly agreed with the statement, while in the other groups only 11 percent of Group C(3), 10 percent of Group B(2), and 8 percent of Group A(1) strongly agreed.

There was a high degree of unanimity across groups that producing a child does *not* prove that a person is sexually mature. Those who strongly disagreed with the premise totaled 86 percent. Only 18 people (3 percent) altogether strongly agreed, and they were mainly in Groups C(3) and D(4).

There was near unanimity across groups also with respect to leaving to chance or Providence the choice to have children. Nearly 86 percent of all respondents strongly disagreed with the statement: 87 percent of Group A(1), 90 percent of Groups B(2) and C(3), and 77 percent of Group D(4).

With respect to the statement that married couples should have the right to choose how many children to have, if any, 76 percent of all respondents strongly agreed, and an additional 15 percent agreed with reservations. A total of 20 people (less than 4 percent) strongly disagreed with this statement and 23 others (4 percent) disagreed with reservations.

The statement "There ought to be available some kind of socially acceptable legal 'divorce' for parents from children who have grown unmanageable but not sufficiently delinquent to be made wards of a court" provoked strong disagreement by 45 percent of all respondents, evenly apportioned across groups. Another 16 percent of all respondents also disagreed, but with reservations. Over 17 percent agreed with the statement with reservations; over 22 percent of Group A(1) respondents were in this group. Twenty-three people (4 percent) strongly agreed with the statement, 11 (2 percent) of whom were in Group D(4).

Attitudes on Family Decisions and Disagreements

Data concerning attitudes on family decisions and disagreements can be found in Table 30. Approximately 43 percent of respondents in Groups B(2), C(3), and D(4), and 32 percent of those in Group A(1) strongly disagreed with the statement "Family decisions should be arrived at democratically, with each member, including children as young as four years, having equal vote." Over 31 percent of all respondents disagreed with reservations; slightly over 19 percent agreed with reservations; and only 7 percent strongly agreed.

About 37 percent of respondents strongly disagreed that family decisions should be arrived at by equal vote of only those members over 12 years of age, and an equal percentage disagreed with reservations. The percentages across all age groups were nearly equal. Almost 20 percent of all respondents agreed with the statement, but with reservations. Only 4 percent strongly agreed.

Nearly 47 percent of the respondents strongly agreed that parents should share equally in making decisions concerning family life-style, money, job selection, home location, schools, etc. Over 36 percent agreed with reservations. Of those respondents strongly agreeing, 22 percent were in Group A(1), 25 percent in Group B(2), 30 percent in Group C(3), and 23 percent in Group D(4). Only 6 percent of all groups strongly disagreed with this statement.

With respect to the statement "If parents can't come to agreement on family decisions, the father should have the final word," 45 percent of the respondents were in strong disagreement. About 23 percent of these respondents were in Group A(1), 34 percent in Group B(2), 25 percent in Group C(3), and only 18 percent were in Group D(4). (About a third of those strongly agreeing were also in Group D(4).) About 19 percent of Groups A(1), B(2), and C(3) and 26 percent of Group D(4) disagreed with reservations. Of the 21 percent of the respondents agreeing with reservations, 38 percent were in Group D(4) and 35 percent were in Group C(3). Less than 10 percent were in Group A(1).

Fifty-five percent of all respondents strongly disagreed that in serious disagreements the father's method of child training and discipline should prevail, and another 24 percent disagreed with reservations. Slightly over 13 percent of the respondents agreed with reservations, and only 4 percent strongly agreed. Of the total respondents strongly disagreeing with this statement, 22 percent were in Group A(1), 31 percent in Group B(2), 29 percent in Group C(3), and only 18 percent were in Group D(4).

The percentage of respondents (47.4) that strongly disagreed that in serious disagreements the mother's way should prevail was smaller than the percentage that strongly disagreed that the father's way should prevail, and a higher percentage (33.1) disagreed with reservations. The same percentage — slightly over 13 percent — agreed with reservations, and only 2 percent of the respondents strongly agreed that the mother's way should prevail, half of whom were in Group B(2).

Forty percent of all respondents strongly agreed that parents should call in outside counsel as soon as possible when agreement cannot be reached about basic methods of child training and discipline. Slightly over 32 percent of these were in Group D(4), 29 percent in Group C(3), 23 percent in Group B(2), and only 16 percent in Group A(1). Over 35 percent of all respondents agreed with this statement with reservations, the highest percentage of whom (32.2) were in Group B(2). Only 8 percent strongly disagreed, and 12 percent disagreed with reservations.

Attitudes Toward Rules for Rearing Children

From the data presented in Tables 31, 32, 33, and 34, attitudes toward rules for rearing children can be determined. At least 65 percent of respondents in all groups strongly agreed that punishment of children should not be severe but should be swift and certain. At least another 25 percent of all respondents agreed with reservations. Over 70 percent of all groups strongly agreed that more time should be spent praising children than showing disapproval; around 20 percent agreed with reservations.

There were mixed responses to the statement concerning the discussion of infractions with children; however, at least 17 percent of all groups strongly agreed that infractions should be discussed at length, even with toddlers. In Group A(1), 38 percent strongly agreed; in Group B(2), 23 percent; in Group C(3), 17 percent; and in Group D(4), 24 percent. Those who agreed with reservations comprised 34 percent of Group A(1), 36 percent of Group B(2), 37 percent of Group C(3), and 28 percent of Group D(4).

The statement that rules made, if reasonable, should not be changed elicited strong disagreement, as follows: 31 percent of Group A(1), 30 percent of Group B(2), 31 percent of Group C(3), and 20 percent of Group D(4). Approximately as many respondents disagreed with reservations as agreed with reservations. Those who disagreed with reservations made up 27 percent of Group A(1), 28 percent of Group B(2), 32 percent of Group C(3), and 35 percent of Group D(4). Those who agreed with reservations made up 32 percent of Group A(1), 30 percent of Group B(2), 30 percent of Group C(3), and 34 percent of Group D(4). Forty-three of a total of 516 respondents (8 percent) strongly agreed that reasonable rules should not be changed: 7, 13, 9, and 14 respondents from Groups A(1), B(2), C(3), and D(4) respectively.

Sixty percent of 514 respondents strongly disagreed with the statement that rules should be few and fully explained, but reasons for making them should not be given: 71 percent of Group A(1), 67 percent of Group B(2), 59 percent of Group C(3), and 47 percent of Group D(4). Those who disagreed with reservations were 17 percent of Group A(1), 22 percent of Group B(2), 29 percent of Group C(3), and 23 percent of Group D(4). Fifty-nine people (11 percent) agreed with the statement with reservations: 5 in Group A(1), 8 in Group B(2), 12 in Group C(3), and 34 in Group D(4). Twenty-one respondents (4 percent) strongly agreed with the statement: 5 in Group A(1), 5 in Group B(2), 4 in Group C(3), and 7 in Group D(4).

Only 9 respondents (less than 2 percent) showed any disagreement with the statement that parental honesty is crucial, that hypocrisy cannot be hidden from children. At least 80 percent of all groups strongly agreed: 80 percent of Group A(1), 84 percent of Group B(2), 81 percent of Group C(3), and 93 percent of Group D(4). Another 13 percent of all respondents agreed with reservations.

With respect to the statement: "Lecturing or warning children is a waste of breath," 30 percent of the respondents strongly disagreed: 45 percent of Group A(1), 34 percent of Group B(2), 27 percent of Group C(3), and 18 percent of Group D(4). More (39 percent) disagreed with reservations: 35 percent of Group A(1), 40 percent of Group B(2), 41 percent of Group C(3), and 38 percent of Group D(4). A total of 26 percent agreed with the statement, with reservations: 13 percent of Group A(1), 22 percent of Group B(2), 27 percent of Group C(3), and 38 percent of Group D(4). Only 26 respondents (5 percent) strongly agreed. These strongly affirmative responses were nearly evenly distributed across the four groups.

With the statement concerning no compromise and strict enforcement of rules expressive of basic parental values, 47 percent strongly agreed: 27 percent of Group A(1), 47 percent of Group B(2), 58 percent of Group C(3), and 51 percent of Group C(4). Another 31 percent agreed with reservations: 38 percent of Group A(1), 29 percent of Group B(2), 22 percent of Group C(3), and 37 percent of Group D(4). Thirty-four people (7 percent) strongly disagreed with the statement: 11 in Group A(1), 13 in Group B(2), 7 in Group C(3), and 3 in Group D(4). Sixty-four respondents (12 percent) disagreed with reservations: 20 in Group A(1), 13 in Group B(2), 19 in Group C(3), and 12 in Group D(4).

There were 519 people responding to the statement requiring children, from an early age, to assume responsibility and make their own decisions. Seventy-five percent strongly agreed with this statement: 80 percent of Group A(1), 78 percent of Group B(2), 74 percent of Group C(3), and 70 percent of Group D(4). Another 23 percent of the total agreed with reservations: 19 percent of Group A(1), 19 percent of Group B(2), 23 percent of Group C(3), and 28 percent of Group D(4). There were only 5 people (less than 1 percent) in all the groups indicating any disagreement with the statement.

Concerning the statement that a child should be allowed to follow his own inclinations, barring destructive behavior, 519 people responded. Of these, 27 percent strongly agreed: 41 percent of Group A(1), 35 percent of Group B(2), 22 percent of Group C(3), and 16 percent of Group D(4). Another 40 percent agreed with the statement with reservations: 40 percent of Group A(1), 36 percent of Group B(2), 42 percent of Group C(3), and 42 percent of Group D(4). Sixty-seven respondents (13 percent) strongly disagreed: 9 in Group A(1), 13 in Group B(2), 22 in Group C(3), and 23 in Group D(4). Of the 93 respondents (18 percent) who disagreed with the statement with reservations, 7 were in Group A(1), 24 in Group B(2), 29 in Group C(3), and 33 in Group D(4).

Of the 516 responding to the statement that children should not be expected to show more control than parents, 58 percent strongly agreed, with approximately equal percentages for each group. An additional 24 percent of the respondents agreed with the statement with reservations: 18 percent of Group A(1), 24 percent of Group B(2), 28 percent of Group C(3), and 25 percent of Group D(4). Thirty-three people (6 percent) strongly disagreed with the statement: 9 in Group A(1), 12 in Group B(2), 7 in Group C(3), and 5 in Group D(4). Forty-one respondents (8 percent) disagreed with the statement with reservations: 7 in Group A(1), 9 in Group B(2), 11 in Group C(3), and 14 in Group D(4).

Attributes Valuable for a Child to Develop

Tables 35, 36, 37, 38, and 39, relating to attributes valuable for a child to develop, show that self-sufficiency and good self-image led among the attributes chosen as most valuable or indispensable for a child to develop in order to have a satisfactory life in today's world. Cooperation, adaptability, tolerance, and perseverance were also high on the list.

Factors Important to Child's Self-Image

There was a high response to both statements concerning factors important to children's self-images, as seen in Table 40. Of the 516 people responding to the statement that what is most important to children's self-images is what they think their parents think of them, 92 (18 percent) were in Group A(1), 139 (27 percent) in Group B(2), 148 (29 percent) in

Group C(3), and 137 (27 percent) in Group D(4). Of the 92 people responding in Group A(1), 17 percent strongly disagreed, 11 percent disagreed with reservations, 35 percent agreed with reservations, 29 percent strongly agreed, and 8 percent had no opinion. All of the 139 people in Group B(2) responded to this query. In this group, 8 percent strongly disagreed, 9 percent disagreed with reservations, 38 percent agreed with reservations, 40 percent strongly agreed, and 5 percent had no opinion. Of the 148 people responding in Group C(3), 7 percent strongly disagreed, 14 percent disagreed with reservations, 39 percent agreed with reservations, 34 percent strongly agreed, and 6 percent had no opinion. Of the 137 people responding in Group D(4), 12 percent strongly disagreed, 14 percent disagreed with reservations, 36 percent agreed with reservations, and 38 percent strongly agreed.

Of the 518 people responding to the statement that what is most important to children's self-images is what they think their peers think of them, 93 (18 percent) were in Group A(1), 139 (27 percent) in Group B(2), 148 (28 percent) in Group C(3), and 138 (27 percent) in Group D(4). Of the 93 respondents in Group A(1), 13 percent strongly disagreed, 10 percent disagreed with reservations, 42 percent agreed with reservations, 30 percent strongly agreed, and 5 percent had no opinion. Of the 139 people responding in Group B(2) (all of that group), 9 percent strongly disagreed, 6 percent disagreed with reservations, 44 percent agreed with reservations, 36 percent strongly agreed, and 5 percent had no opinion. Of the 148 people responding in Group C(3), 5 percent strongly disagreed, 9 percent disagreed with reservations, 40 percent agreed with reservations, 41 percent strongly agreed and 5 percent had no opinion. Of the 138 respondents in Group D(4), 7 percent strongly disagreed, 4 percent disagreed with reservations, 39 percent agreed with reservations, 49 percent strongly agreed, and 1 percent had no opinion.

Since most of the people responding to the entire questionnaire answered the two queries in Table 40, it would seem from a comparison of the data that respondents felt that both statements were pertinent and that they were not mutually exclusive.

Reasons Parents Had First Child

Slightly more than half (52 percent) of the respondents to the full questionnaire answered the queries in Table 41 concerning reasons for having their first child. Only one person in Group A(1) responded as a parent with reasons for having a first child. Thirty-three people in Group B(2) responded, with over half giving reasons other than those listed. In Group C(3), 17 percent stated that their first child happened accidentally; 18 percent that they had the child because they felt their marriage would be more complete with a child; 37 percent gave other reasons not on the list; and 20 percent gave multiple reasons. In Group D(4), 14 percent stated that it happened accidentally; 26 percent said to complete their marriage; 31 percent gave other reasons; and 16 percent gave multiple reasons. The reasons for having a first child, listed by respondents in Groups B(2), C(3), and D(4), are presented in the following subsections.

Reasons for Having First Child Other than Those Listed in Questionnaire

The following are some of the reasons for having a first child given by respondents in Group B(2):

1. I (we) wanted a child. (At least five respondents gave this answer.)
2. I wanted the happy and fulfilling experience. *Or*, I wanted the joy a child could give.
3. My wife and I both wanted to carry on productive intelligent people rather than allow the dullards to breed themselves into dominance. *Or*, Good genes.
4. I felt my spouse and I would be in a good position to raise a happy, healthy child who could contribute to the world and to the future. *Or*, I felt my husband and I would make good parents. *Or*, I felt my husband and I had the emotional and financial support necessary to raise a happy, self-sufficient child. *Or*, We were ready for the responsibilities of becoming parents. *Or*, Family was always important to me and my husband, and I was "ready."
5. I wanted to be a part of the purpose of earth life — to raise a child and create the beginning of an eternal family.
6. I love children — I wanted to give someone else the happy childhood I had. *Or*, We wanted to share our life with someone else. *Or*, We wanted to give someone else the chance to experience the joys of living.

The following are some of the other reasons for having a first child given by respondents in Group C(3):

1. At least sixteen people stated: I (we) wanted a child. Additional variations of this were: I just plain wanted a family; we wanted a child, period; I just wanted a child to "mother"; and I wanted a child to raise and enjoy.
2. I saw the pleasure other families were having with theirs.
3. At least three people stated simply: I like children. Others stated: I love children and wanted a family. *Or*, I adore children and have

lots of love to share.
4. The girl I was living with decided she wanted another child but did not consult me.
5. I wanted a child to teach me love.
6. I didn't want to not have the experience — having children is a part of life.
7. I had a great desire to share the privilege and responsibility of helping a child mature. *Or,* I wanted to share the experience of being responsible in the growth and development of a child.
8. At least four people stated: We wanted to share our love with a child. Others stated: We wanted the experience and pleasure of sharing our relationship with a child. *Or,* I (we) wanted the joy of teaching and sharing.
9. I (we) wanted the personal satisfaction of a child. *Or,* I (we) wanted the experience of parenthood and giving birth. *Or,* I thought having a child in our home would be fun. *Or,* I've always looked forward to having a family.
10. I felt an inner need for a child. *Or,* I thought my life would be more complete with a child. *Or,* We felt a really basic desire for children and a family life-style we felt happiest with. *Or,* I wanted to live with children, raise them, and enjoy their personalities and contributions.
11. I wanted to give someone else the happy childhood I had.
12. At least two people stated: We wanted children because we love them and because we knew we would be good parents. Others stated: We wanted a child and felt we could bear and rear healthy and happy children of our own. We believe in ourselves and felt we should enhance society by having a child with our belief and morals.
13. I was ready to assume the responsibility and to enjoy the child.
14. We wanted a child and my husband was concerned with having "a son and heir."

The following are some of the other reasons for having a first child given by respondents in Group D(4):

1. At least eight people gave as their reason for having a first child: I (we) wanted a child. An additional similar response: I wanted children — period. At least two responded: I love children and wanted some of my own. At least three people stated simply: I love children, and three stated: I like children. Others stated: I wanted to have children to love and raise.
2. We had always considered having a family. *Or,* We just felt it

would be nice to have a child. *Or,* It was something we both wanted to share.

3. It never occurred to me not to have children—I always wanted five or six. *Or,* I never thought of not having children.
4. I felt life would be more meaningful and happy with children. *Or,* I felt my life would be more complete with children. *Or,* We like family life and it isn't complete without children.
5. That's what life is all about. *Or,* We wanted children because we felt it was fulfillment of life (ego?).
6. No birth control method was used.
7. I had an innate desire to have a family. *Or,* I have strong maternal instincts.
8. I wanted to create a new person—raise a useful, happy person—with the help of my husband.
9. I wanted the experience. *Or,* I wanted the experience of raising children.
10. All my friends were having babies.
11. I desired the experience of producing another life and helping that life find meaning and fulfillment. *Or,* I wanted to mold an individual. *Or,* I wanted to have children to bring up and educate.
12. I wanted someone else to enjoy the experience of the world.
13. I wanted a child and we could give it a good home and be good parents.
14. My husband and I like children and wanted to give our children a "good" home life; we also wanted to continue the family with a "next generation."
15. We thought healthy, intelligent people should have children to maintain the human race. We really believe college people should have four children.

Respondents Using Questionnaire List
but Giving Multiple Reasons

The totals in the category "multiple reasons" were in addition to the single reason categories. Although most of the multiple answers included also the reasons listed, they were tallied separately. Thus, the single reason categories could be increased slightly by including the appropriate parts of the multiple responses.

There were only five people in Group B(2) giving multiple reasons for having a first child. Two of the multiple reason combinations given were:

1. I felt my marriage would be more complete with a child/I wanted

to please my mate. (This reason was given by two respondents.)

2. I felt my marriage would be more compete with a child/I wanted to give someone else the happy childhood I had.

The multiple reasons given by respondents in Group C(3) were 20 percent of all responses in that group. Some of the multiple reason combinations given were:

1. I felt my marriage would be more complete with a child/I wanted to please my mate. (This reason was given by at least two respondents.)
2. I felt my marriage would be more complete with a child/I wanted to please my mate/I thought that's what was expected in marriage. (This reason was given by at least two respondents.)
3. I felt my marriage would be more complete with a child/it happened accidentally.
4. I wanted to please my mate, it happened accidentally/I thought that's what was expected in marriage.
5. I felt my marriage would be more complete with a child/I thought that's what was expected in marriage. (This reason was given by at least three respondents.)
6. I felt my marriage would be more complete with a child/I wanted something of my very own to take care of and have the say about.
7. Because of religious convictions/I wanted something of my very own to take care of and have the say about.
8. It happened accidentally/I wanted to please my mate.
9. It happened accidentally/I felt my marriage would be more complete with a child/I thought a child would save my faltering marriage.

The multiple reasons given by respondents in Group D(4) were 16 percent of all responses in that group. Some of the multiple reason combinations given were:

1. I thought that's what was expected in marriage/I wanted something of my very own to take care of and have the say about/I felt my marriage would be more complete with a child/I wanted to please my mate.
2. I thought that's what was expected in marriage/It happened accidentally/I felt my marriage would be more complete with a child.
3. I wanted something of my very own to take care of and have the

say about/I wanted to give someone else the happy childhood I didn't have/I felt my marriage would be more complete with a child.
4. I thought that's what was expected in marriage/I wanted to give someone else the happy childhood I didn't have/I felt my marriage would be more complete with a child.
5. I thought that's what was expected in marriage/I wanted to please my mate/I felt my marriage would be more complete with a child.
6. It happened accidentally/I felt my marriage would be more complete with a child. (At least two respondents gave this combination of reasons.)
7. It happened accidentally/I thought that's what was expected in marriage.
8. I felt my marriage would be more complete with a child/I wanted to please my mate.

Reasons Parents Had Second Child

Slightly more than 40 percent of the respondents to the full questionnaire answered the queries in Table 42 about reasons for having a second child. Of these, 8 people were in Group B(2), 90 in Group C(3), and 113 in Group D(4). There were none in Group A(1).

Twenty-five (12 percent) of the total respondents to this question gave as their reason for having a second child, "It happened accidentally." Of these, 2 were in Group B(2), 11 in Group C(3), and 12 in Group D(4).

Well over half (54 percent) of the respondents to this question gave as their reason for having a second child, "I wanted my child to have brother(s), sister(s)." Of this 54 percent, only 1 percent was in Group B(2), 42 percent were in Group C(3), and 57 percent were in Group D(4).

There were only 91 people who responded to the question why they had a third child, and 29 who responded why they had a fourth or subsequent children. Again, the reason most often given was "I wanted my children to have brother(s), sister(s)," The second most frequent reason given was "It happened accidentally."

Reasons for Not Having Children

Only 30 people in all groups gave reasons why they were deterred from having a first child. Only 34 responded with reasons why they were deterred from having a second child. There were 68 responses with reasons for being deterred from having a fourth child.

Although several reasons were on the questionnaire list for not having children (e.g., the possibility of nuclear war, unstable national or global economic conditions), the chief reasons given by the respondents were the high cost of raising children and the disinclination to add to an overpopulated world. Respondents also added reasons of their own that were not listed in the questionnaire. Figures for these latter reasons and for the two most frequently stated reasons (the high cost of raising children and overpopulation) are given in Table 43.

There were only three responses from Group A(1) giving reasons for not having a first, second, third, or fourth child. Since the respondents in Group A(1) were age 25 or younger, and most had not had children, this was to be expected. Of the three people from Group A(1) responding to reasons for not having a first child, one person gave the possibility of nuclear war and two people gave other reasons of their own not on the questionnaire list.

Group B(2) was represented by only 8 people with reasons deterring them from having a first child. Seven people from Group B(2) gave reasons for not having a second child, 11 people for not having a third child, and 6 people for not having a fourth child. Thus, Groups C(3) and D(4), with total responses of 89 and 59 respectively, representing all reasons given with respect to a first, second, third, and fourth child, are the groups of chief interest in Table 43. This table gives only the most frequently stated reasons for not having children, namely; the high cost of raising children, overpopulation, and a combination of respondents' personal reasons not on the questionnaire list.

Of the total respondents answering the query regarding reasons for not having a first child, 23 percent gave the high cost of raising a child as the reason. A like percentage of respondents gave high cost as the reason for not having a fourth child. The percentage of respondents giving high cost as the reason for not having a second or third child was 26 percent.

Only 7 percent of those answering the query regarding reasons for not having a first child gave overpopulation as a reason. The percentage of respondents giving overpopulation as the reason for not having a second child was 15 percent; for not having a third child, 26 percent; and for not having a fourth child, 23 percent.

The percentages of respondents giving a combination of reasons not on the questionnaire list for not having children were fairly substantial: 40 percent of those answering with respect to a first child, 38 percent with respect to a second child, 26 percent with respect to a third child, and 30 percent with respect to a fourth child.

Parental Opinions Concerning Children as Hindrances

As indicated by Table 44, except for the category of job selection, children were, at least "to small degree," a hindrance to the pursuits listed for at least 20 percent of the total respondents. Only 11 percent of the total respondents found children a hindrance to a small degree in job selection.

Of the 235 people answering the query concerning job selection 2 (1 percent) were in Group A(1), 28 (12 percent) in Group B(2), 106 (45 percent) in Group C(3), and 99 (42 percent) in Group D(4). Of the 28 in Group B(2), 22 people (79 percent) stated that children were "not at all" a hindrance, 1 person (less than 4 percent) stated "to a small degree," 1 (less than 4 percent) stated "to a moderate degree," 2 (7 percent) stated "to a high degree," and 2 (7 percent) stated "very definitely." Of the 106 people responding in Group C(3), 65 people (61 percent) stated that children were "not at all" a hindrance, 14 (13 percent) stated "to a small degree," 13 (12 percent) stated "to a moderate degree," 7 (7 percent) stated "to a high degree," and 6 (6 percent) stated "very definitely." Of the 99 responding in Group D(4), 70 people (71 percent) indicated children were "not at all" a hindrance in job selection, 10 (10 percent) indicated "to a small degree," 8 (8 percent) stated "to a moderate degree," 3 (3 percent) stated "to a high degree," and 4 (4 percent) stated "very definitely."

Of the 245 replying to the query concerning travel opportunities, 2 (less than 1 percent) were in Group A(1), 29 (12 percent) in Group B(2), 108 (44 percent) in Group C(3), and 106 (43 percent) in Group D(4). Of the 29 in Group B(2), 5 (17 percent) stated that children were "not at all" a hindrance to their travel opportunities, 9 (31 percent) stated "to a small degree," 6 (21 percent) stated "to a moderate degree," 5 (17 percent) stated "to a high degree," and 4 (14 percent) stated "very definitely." Of the 108 respondents in Group C(3), 20 people (19 percent) stated "not at all," 28 (26 percent) stated "to a small degree," 28 (26 percent) stated "to a moderate degree," 20 (19 percent) stated "to a high degree," and 10 (9 percent) stated "very definitely." Of the 106 respondents in Group D(4), 41 people (39 percent) stated children were "not at all" a hindrance, 28 (26 percent) stated "to a small degree," 20 (19 percent stated "to a moderate degree," 12 (11 percent) stated "to a high degree," and 3 (3 percent) stated "very definitely."

Of the 247 people replying to the query regarding general mobility, 3 (1 percent) were in Group A(1), 29 (12 percent) in Group B(2), 112 (45 percent) in Group C(3), and 103 (42 percent) in Group D(4). Of the 29 in Group B(2), 2 people (7 percent) stated children were "not at all" a hindrance to their mobility, 9 (31 percent) stated "to a small degree," 11 (38 percent) stated "to a moderate degree," 4 (14 percent) stated "to a high degree," and 3 (10 percent) stated "very definitely." Of the 112 in Group C(3), 30 people (27 percent) indicated children were "not at all" a hindrance, 21 (19 percent) stated "to a small degree," 33 (29 percent) stated "to a moderate degree," 16 (14 percent) stated "to a high degree," and 10 (9 percent) stated "very definitely." Of the 103 responding in Group D(4), 50 people (49 percent) stated children were "not at all" a hindrance, 30 (29 percent) stated "to a small degree," 14 (14 percent) stated "to a moderate degree," 6 (6 percent) stated "to a high degree," and 2 (2 percent) stated "very definitely."

Of the 253 people responding to the query as to whether children were a hindrance to saving money, 2 (less than 1 percent) were in Group A(1), 30 (12 percent) in Group B(2), 110 (43 percent) in Group C(3), and 111 (44 percent) in Group D(4). Of the 30 in Group B(2), 3 people (10 percent) stated children were "not at all" a hindrance, 11 (37 percent) stated "to a small degree," 6 (20 percent) stated "to a moderate degree," 5 (17 percent) stated "to a high degree," and 4 (13 percent) stated "very definitely." Of the 110 responding in Group C(3), 30 people (27 percent) stated "not at all," 28 (25 percent) stated "to a small degree," 28 (25 percent) stated "to a moderate degree," 12 (11 percent) stated "to a high degree," and 11 (10 percent) stated "very definitely." Of the 111 respondents in Group D(4), 21 people (19 percent) stated children were "not at all" a hindrance, 28 (25 percent) stated "to a small degree," 31 (28 percent) stated "to a moderate degree," 21 (19 percent) stated "to a high degree," and 10 (9 percent) stated "very definitely."

Of the 240 people responding to the query regarding children as a hindrance to staying out of debt, 2 (less than 1 percent) were in Group A(1), 30 (13 percent) in Group B(2), 103 (43 percent) in Group C(3), and 105 (44 percent) in Group D(4). Of the 30 in Group B(2), 16 people (53 percent) stated that children were "not at all" a hindrance, 6 people (20 percent) stated "to a small degree," 4 (13 percent) stated "to a moderate degree," and 1 (3 percent) each stated "to a high degree" and "very definitely." Of the 103 respondents in Group C(3), 58 people (56 percent) stated that children were "not at all" a hindrance, 17 (17 percent) stated "to a small degree," 16 (16 percent) stated "to a moderate degree," 6 (6 percent) stated "to a high degree," and 4 (4 percent) stated "very definitely." Of the 105 respondents in Group D(4), 46 people (44 percent) indicated children were "not at all" a hindrance to their staying out of debt, 27 (26 percent) stated "to a small degree," 14 (13 percent) stated "to a moderate degree," and 7 and 8 people (7 and 8 percent) respectively, stated "to a high degree" and "very definitely."

Of the 251 respondents to the query concerning children as a hindrance to having free time for personal pursuits, 2 (less than 1 percent) were in Group A(1), 29 (12 percent) in Group B(2), 114 (45 percent) in Group C(3), and 106 (42 percent) in Group D(4). Of the 29 in Group B(2), 3 (10 percent) stated that children were "not at all" a hindrance, 5 (17 percent) stated "to a small degree," 10 (34 percent) stated "to a moderate degree," 8 (28 percent) stated "to a high degree," and 3 (10 percent) stated "very definitely." Of the 114 in Group C(3), only 8 people (7 percent) stated that children were "not at all" a hindrance, 31 (27 percent) indicated "to a small degree," 30 (26 percent) stated "to a moderate degree," 27 (24 per cent) stated "to a high degree," and 16 (14 percent) stated "very definitely." Of the 106 respondents in Group D(4), 25 people (24 percent) stated children were "not at all" a hindrance, 35 (33 percent) stated "to a small degree," 29 (27 percent) stated "to a moderate degree," 12 (11 percent) stated "to a high degree," and 5 (5 percent) stated "very definitely."

Disagreements Between Adults in Home over Children

Table 45 indicates that 44 percent of respondents to this question stated that 10 percent of disagreements between spouses or other adults in the home were due to the children of the household. About 90 percent of these respondents were fairly equally divided between Groups C(3) and D(4).

A little more than 17 percent of all respondents to this question gave children as the cause for 20 percent of such disagreements. Again, about 89 percent of these respondents were about equally divided between Groups C(3) and D(4).

Almost 12 percent of all respondents to this question gave children as the cause for 50 percent of such disagreements. Again, 84 percent of these respondents were divided about equally between Groups C(3) and D(4).

Thirteen people, or 5 percent, stated the children of the household were the cause of more than 50 percent of such disagreements. Eight of these were in Group D(4) and 3 in Group C(3).

Causes of Disagreements over Children

Table 46 contains information with respect to causes of household disagreements over children. "Differences regarding children's behavioral training" was given as the cause of disagreements over children by 132 respondents: 2 (2 percent) in Group A(1), 17 (13 percent) in Group B(2), 61 (46 percent) in Group C(3), and 52 (39 percent) in Group D(4). "Differences as to methods of correction" was stated as a cause by 128 respondents: 3 (2 percent) in Group A(1), 11 (9 percent) in Group B(2), 68 (53 percent) in Group C(3), and 46 (36 percent) in Group D(4).

"Money difficulties involving costs of raising children" was given as a cause by 25 people: 2 (8 percent) in Group B(2), 9 (36 percent) in Group C(3), and 14 (56 percent) in Group D(4). "Feelings of incapacity to cope with recalcitrant children" was stated as a cause by 23 respondents: 1 (4 percent) in Group A(1), 14 (61 percent) in Group C(3), and 8 (35 percent) in Group D(4). "School troubles" was given as a cause by 17 people: 1 (6 percent) each in Groups A(1) and B(2), 2 (12 percent) in Group C(3), and 13 (76 percent) in Group D(4).

"Differences as to which adult should have the final say about punishment" was stated as a cause by 16 respondents: 1 (6 percent) each in Groups A(1) and B(2), and 7 (44 percent) each in Groups C(3) and D(4). "Troubles with neighbors" was given as a cause by 15 respondents: 5 (33 percent) in Group C(3), and 10 (67 percent) in Group D(4). "Differences regarding children's religious training" was a cause given by 11 people: 7 (64 percent) in Group C(3), and 4 (36 percent) in Group D(4). "Differences about behavior of stepchildren" was given as a cause by 4 people: 1 (25 percent) in Group C(3) and 3 (75 percent) in Group D(4).

Thus, the two causes most frequently given were differences regarding behavioral training and those related to methods of correction. In both instances the highest percentages of affirmative responses were given by Group C(3) (ages 32 through 44.)

Attitudes Toward Influence of Children on Divorce Decisions

In Table 47, of the 86 people responding to the query as to whether or not offspring were a basic cause of conflict leading up to divorce, 47 percent of those divorced had no opinion and 37 percent replied that they felt offspring were not at all a basic source of conflict. Of the people giving the latter response 66 percent were in Group D(4) and 25 percent in Group C(3).

Of the 85 people responding to the query: "If divorced, do you think you would have had the divorce if there were no children in your family?" 45 percent of respondents had no opinion, 14 percent thought they would very likely ("to a high degree") have had the divorce whether or not there were children and 28 percent stated they definitely would have had the divorce whether or not there were children in the family. Both the latter percentages were chiefly represented by Group C(3) and D(4) respondents.

As to the query to those possibly contemplating divorce, "Does a child (children) stand in the way?" 28 percent of the 136 respondents had no opinion, 31 percent answered "not at all," 10 percent replied "to a high degree," and 15 percent stated "very definitely." Of the 14 people indicating a child (children) did stand in the way of a divorce to a high degree, 9 (64 percent) were in Group C(3) and 4 (29 percent) were in Group D(4). Of the 20 stating that a child (children) very definitely stood in the way of a divorce, 12 (60 percent) were in Group C(3) and 4 (20 percent) in Group D(4).

Some Factors Indicating Degree of Parental Attentiveness

Only 30 people in Group B(2) responded to the question, "How much time per day do (did) you spend playing or conversing with your child (children)?" Of these 30 respondents, 25 (83 percent) spent more than one hour, as can be seen in Table 48. Of the 120 people in Group C(3) answering the question, 82 (68 percent) spent more than one hour per day. Of the 118 people responding in Group D(4), 82 (69 percent) spent more than one hour per day.

With respect to babysitters used, only 31 people in Group B(2) responded, one-third of whom used paid outsiders in their homes. There were 118 respondents in Group C(3) to the question of babysitters and 111 respondents in Group D(4). Grandparents were used by (23 percent) in Group D(4), and by only 7 percent in Group C(3). Paid outsiders in respondents' homes were used by 42 percent of respondents in Group C(3) and 36 percent in Group D(4). Combinations of grandparents, other relatives, friends, and paid outsiders were used by 31 percent of respondents in Group C(3) and by 33 percent in Group D(4).

Only 27 people in Group B(2) responded to the queries regarding number of hours per day television was used as a babysitter. Of these, 59 percent stated television was used less than one hour per day. In Group C(3), there were 118 respondents to this question, of which 29 percent used television less than one hour per day, 31 percent used it one hour per day, and 31 percent used it two hours per day. In Group D(4), there were 99 respondents, of which 40 percent used television as babysitter less than one hour per day, 27 percent used it one hour, and 23 percent used it two hours per day.

In answer to the question, "When living with you, does (did) your child (children) under 15 years regularly eat dinner with you?" there were 29 answers from Group B(2) respondents, 24 of whom (83 percent) replied affirmatively. Of the 118 responses from Group C(3) and the 119 from Group D(4), 111 (94 percent) and 115 (97 percent), respectively, were affirmative.

In answer to the question as to whether or not children under 15 years of age had regular, specific chores, the 26 respondents in Group B(2) were divided: 13 (50 percent) stated such children had regular, specific chores, and 13 (50 percent) stated they did not. Of the 114 people answering this question in Group C(3), 99 (87 percent) stated their child (children) did have regular, specific chores, and of the 118 respondents in Group D(4), 112 (95 percent) answered affirmatively.

Questions Intended to Elicit Reflective
Importance of Children

As Table 49 shows, only 4 parents from Group A(1) and 29 from Group B(2) responded to the question concerning getting comfort from talking over parent child troubles with another person. Of the 29 in Group B(2), 17 percent stated "not at all," 28 percent "to a moderate degree," 14 percent "to a high degree," and 24 percent "very definitely."

Most respondents to this query were in Groups C(3) and D(4), with 116 and 111 answers, respectively. Of those in Group C(3), 16 percent answered "to a small degree"; 19 percent, "to a moderate degree"; 22 percent , "to a high degree"; and 30 percent, "very definitely." Of those in Group D(4), 26 percent stated they got comfort "to a small degree"; 36 percent, "to a moderate degree"; 11 percent, "to a high degree"; and 14 percent, "very definitely."

Of the 277 respondents to the query concerning the degrees of satisfaction obtained by having obedient children, 5 (2 percent) were in Group A(1), 33 (12 percent) in Group B(2), 123 (44 percent) in Group C(3) and 116 (42 percent) in Group D(4). Of those in Group B(2), 15 percent had no opinion; 12 percent stated "to a small degree"; 21 percent, "to a moderate degree"; 33 percent, "to a high degree"; and 18 percent, "very definitely." Of those in Group C(3), 28 percent indicated satisfaction in having obedient children "to a moderate degree"; 33 percent," to a high degree"; and 30 percent, "very definitely." Of those in Group D(4) indicating such satisfaction, 12 percent stated "to a small degree"; 37 percent, "to a moderate degree"; 32 percent, "to a high degree"; and 17 percent, "very definitely."

Of the 275 respondents to the query, "Do you take personal satisfaction in being told your child (children) is (are) attractive, talented or well mannered?" 4 (1 percent) were in Group A(1), 33 (12 percent) in Group B(2), 122 (44 percent) in Group C(3), and 116 (42 percent) in Group D(4). Of those in Group B(2), 24 percent stated they took personal satisfaction "to a moderate degree"; 36 percent, "to a high degree"; and 27 percent, "very definitely." Of those in Group C(3), 18 percent took satisfaction "to a moderate degree"; 34 percent, "to a high degree"; and 43 percent, "very definitely." Of the 116 in Group D(4), 27 percent indicated they took satisfaction "to a moderate degree"; 35 percent, "to a high degree"; and 33 percent, "very definitely."

Of the 280 respondents to the query, "Does it give you pleasure to be known as someone's mother or father?" 4 (1 percent) were in Group A(1), 34 (12 percent) in Group B(2), 123 (44 percent) in Group C(3), and 119 (43 percent) in Group D(4). Of the 34 in Group B(2), 18 percent answered "to a small degree"; 21 percent, "to a moderate degree"; 26 percent, "to a high degree"; and 26 percent, "very definitely." Of those in Group C(3), 24 percent stated "to a moderate degree"; 27 percent, "to a high degree"; and 37 percent, "very definitely," Of those in Group D(4), 24 percent gave affirmative answers to "to a moderate degree"; 27 percent, "to a high degree"; and 39 percent, "very definitely."

As to the question; "Do you feel personally triumphant in your offspring's accomplishments?" there were 277 respondents: 4 (1 percent) in

Group A(1), 33 (12 percent) in Group B(2), 121 (44 percent) in Group C(3), and 119 (43 percent) in Group D(4). Of those in Group B(2), 12 percent stated they did not feel at all personally triumphant; 27 percent stated "to a small degree"; 33 percent, "to a moderate degree"; 6 percent, "to a high degree"; and 12 percent, "very definitely." Of those in Group C(3), 19 percent indicated they felt personally triumphant "to a small degree"; 30 percent, "to a moderate degree"; 25 percent, "to a high degree"; and 21 percent, "very definitely." Of those in Group D(4), 18 percent stated "to a small degree"; 39 percent, "to a moderate degree"; 19 percent, "to a high degree"; and 19 percent, "very definitely."

Of the 275 responding to the query concerning whether they thought of children as interesting projects to direct, 4 (1 percent) were in Group A(1), 34 (12 percent) in Group B(2), 121 (44 percent) in Group C(3)and 116 (42 percent) in Group D(4). Of those in Group B(2), 41 percent indicated they did "not at all" think of their children as interesting projects; 12 percent stated "to a small degree"; 26 percent, "to a moderate degree"; 6 percent, "to a high degree"; and 6 percent, "very definitely." Of those in Group C(3), 44 percent stated "not at all"; 18 percent, "to a small degree"; 17 percent, "to a moderate degree,"; 14 percent, "to a high degree"; and 5 percent, "very definitely." Of those in Group D(4), 53 percent stated "not at all"; 13 percent, "to a small degree"; 16 percent "to a moderate degree"; 9 percent, "to a high degree"; and 5 percent, "very definitely."

Of the 286 responding to the query, "Do you feel that successful children add to one's status in the community or among friends?" 9 (3 percent) were in Group A(1), 36 (13 percent) in Group B(2), 122 (43 percent) in Group C(3), and 119 (41 percent) in Group D(4). Of those in Group B(2), 14 percent stated "not at all"; 22 percent, "to a small degree"; 33 percent, "to a moderate degree"; 14 percent, "to a high degree"; and 8 percent, "very definitely." Of those in Group C(3), 24 percent stated they thought successful children added to parental status "not at all"; 33 percent stated "to a small degree"; 20 percent, "to a moderate degree"; 12 percent, "to a high degree"; and 7 percent, "very definitely." Of those in Group D(4), 14 percent stated "not at all"; 32 percent, "to a small degree"; 25 percent, "to a moderate degree"; 15 percent, "to a high degree"; and 11 percent, "very definitely."

Of the 287 people responding to the question, "Do you feel you would be missing something important to your personal development if you didn't have at least one child?" 6 (2 percent) were in Group A(1), 38 (13 percent) in Group B(2), 123 (43 percent) in Group C(3), and 120 (42 percent) in Group D(4). At least 52 percent of Groups B(2), C(3), and D(4) felt they would "very definitely" be missing something important to their personal development. Of those responding in Group B(2), 11 percent answered "not at all"; 21 percent, "to a moderate degree"; 13 percent, "to a high degree"; and 53 percent, "very definitely." Of those responding in Group C(3), 11 percent gave the answer "not at all"; 11 percent, "to a small degree"; 9 percent, "to a moderate degree"; 15 percent, "to a high degree"; and 54 percent, "very definitely." Of those responding in Group D(4), 9 percent stated "not at all"; 3 percent, "to a small degree"; 10 percent, "to a moderate degree"; 18 percent, "to a high degree"; and 58 percent, "very definitely."

Of the 285 answering the query, "Do you believe people should sacrifice for their children?" 8 (3 percent) were in Group A(1), 37 (13 percent) in Group B(2), 121 (42 percent) in Group C(3), and 119 (42 percent) in Group D(4). Of those in Group B(2), 8 percent stated "not at all"; 19 percent, "to a small degree"; 43 percent, "to a moderate degree"; 14 percent, "to a high degree"; and 16 percent, "very definitely." Of those in Group C(3), 2 percent stated "not at all"; 16 percent, "to a small degree"; 45 percent, "to a moderate degree"; 20 percent, "to a high degree"; and 17 percent, "very definitely." Of those responding in Group D(4), 4 percent stated "not at all"; 10 percent, "to a small degree"; 50 percent, "to a moderate degree"; 17 percent, "to a high degree"; and 18 percent, "very definitely."

Of the 172 people answering the query, "When your child(children) is (was) grossly disobedient, do (did) you take it as an affront to your right as a parent?" 2 (1 percent) were in Group A(1), 19 (11 percent) in Group B(2), 79 (46 percent) in Group C(3) and 72 (42 percent) in Group D(4). Of those in Group B(2), 58 percent stated "not at all"; 11 percent, "to a small degree"; and 21 percent, "to a moderate degree." Of those in Group C(3), 51 percent answered "not at all"; 20 percent, "to a small degree"; and 14 percent, "to a moderate degree." Of those in Group D(4), 54 percent answered "not at all"; 17 percent, "to a small degree"; 13 percent, "to a moderate degree"; and 14 percent, "to a high degree." Only four people answered "very definitely," 2 of whom were in Group C(3) and 2 in Group D(4).

Of the 200 people responding to the query as to whether gross disobedience in a child was sign of parental failure, 2 (1 percent) were in Group A(1), 20 (10 percent) in Group B(2), 86 (43 percent) in Group C(3), and 92 (46 percent) in Group D(4). Of those in Group B(2), 40 percent indicated they felt such disobedience was "not at all" a sign of their failure as a parent; 15 percent felt it was "to a small degree"; 20 percent, "to a moderate degree"; 10 percent, "to a high degree"; and 10 percent, "very definitely." Of those in Group C(3), 36 percent answered "not at all"; 17 percent , "to a small degree"; 23 percent, "to a moderate degree"; 13 percent, "to a high degree"; and only 5 percent, "very definitely." Of those in Group D(4), 32 percent answered "not at all"; 26 percent, "to a small degree"; 22 percent, "to a moderate degree"; 17 percent, "to a high degree"; and only 3 percent, "very definitely."

As Table 49 shows, responses from Group A(1) were so few in number that in most instances comment on their percentages seemed unwarranted. It should be noted also that responses from Group B(2) were relatively few compared to those made by Groups C(3) and D(4), which consisted of older people with possibly broader parental experience.

Responses to "If You Had It to Do Over Again . . ."

Table 50 gives responses to the question made famous by Ann Landers, "If you had it to over again, would you have had children?" Of the 275 people responding to this question (52.4 percent of all respondents to the questionnaire), only 1 person (less than 1 percent) was in Group A(1), 33 (12 percent) were in Group B(2), and 121 and 120 (44 percent each) respectively, were in Groups C(3) and D(4).

Of those responding, 170 (or 62 percent) would have the number of children they did have if they had it to do over again. Of these, 41 percent were in Group C(3) and 45 percent were in Group D(4). Approximately 16 percent of those responding would have only two children. Of these, 44 percent were in Group C(3) and 53 percent were in Group D(4).

Those undecided were 12 percent of respondents to this question, of which 22 percent were in Group B(2), 41 percent were in Group C(3), and 38 percent were in Group D(4). Only 4 percent of the respondents stated they would not have any children of they had it to do over again, two-thirds of them in Group C(3).

Parental Expectations with Respect to
Dependence on Children

Of the 272 parents responding to the query shown in Table 51, concerning expectations that their children will stay close to them in their old age, 4 (1 percent) were in Group A(1), 33 (12 percent) in Group B(2), 118 (43 percent) in Group C(3), and 117 (43 percent) in Group D(4). The answers from Group A(1) were evenly divided: 50 percent "yes" and 50 percent "no." Of the 33 responding in Group B(2), 73 percent stated that they expected their children to remain close to them and 27 percent responded that they did not. Of the 118 in Group C(3), 72 percent had such expectations and 28 percent did not, and of the 117 in Group D(4), 65 percent had such expectations and 35 percent did not. Thus, in Groups B(2), C(3), and D(4), parental expectations were high that their children would remain close to them in their later years.

Of the 279 parents responding to the query, also shown in Table 51, "Do you depend on their taking care of you when you are old?" 4 (1 percent were in Group A(1), 33 (12 percent) in Group B(2), 122 (44 percent) in Group C(3) and 120 (43 percent) in Group D(4). Over 95 percent of all respondents stated they did *not* depend on their children's taking care of them in old age. In fact, only 14 people (5 percent) indicated that they *did* depend on being taken care of in their old age by their children. One of these respondents was in Group A(1), one in Group B(2), 7 in Group C(3), and 5 in Group D(4).

Attitudes of Female Parents Toward Childbearing

There were 303 female respondents to the entire questionnaire. Approximately half of them answered the queries in Table 52 concerning attitudes toward childbearing, all of them in Groups B(2), C(3), and D(4); there were no responses to these queries from Group A(1).

Of the 162 women responding to the question, "Is (was) your desire to have a child (children) prompted by wanting 'something to do?' " 18 (11 percent) were in Group B(2), 74 (46 percent) in Group C(3), and 70 (43 percent) in Group D(4). More than 87 percent of the respondents did "not at all" desire a child in order to have something to do. In Group B(2), 14 (78 percent) of the 18 women answering stated "not at all"; 2 (11 percent), "to a small degree"; 1 (6 percent), "to a moderate degree"; and one (6 percent), "to a high degree." Of the 74 women responding in Group C(3), 65 (88 percent) stated "not at all"; 5 (7 percent) women stated "to a small degree"; 1 (1 percent), "to a moderate degree"; 2 (3 percent), "to a high degree"; and 1 (1 percent), "very definitely." Of the 70 women answering in Group D(4), 63 (90 percent) indicated they did "not at all" desire a child in order to have something to do; 4 (6 percent) did "to a small degree"; 2 (3 percent), "to a moderate degree"; and 1 (1 percent), "to a high degree."

Of the 160 women answering the query, "Was pregnancy your finest hour?" 19 (12 percent) were in Group B(2), 71 (44 percent) in Group C(3), and 70 (44 percent) in Group D(4). Of the 19 in Group B(2), 5 (26 percent) answered "not at all"; 5 (26 percent), "to a small degree"; 7 (37 percent), "to a moderate degree"; and 2 (11 percent), "to a high degree." Of the 71 in Group C(3), 3 (4 percent) had no opinion; 34 (48 percent) answered "not at all"; 16 (23 percent) stated "to a small degree"; 4 (6 percent), "to a moderate degree"; 10 (14 percent), "to a high degree"; and 4 (6 percent), "very definitely." Of the 70 in Group D(4), 31 (44 percent) answered "not at all"; 15 (21 percent), "to a small degree"; 14 (20 percent), "to a moderate degree"; 8 (11 percent), "to a high degree"; and 2 (3 percent), "very definitely."

Of the 159 women responding to the query as to whether they "needed" to be pregnant "every so often," 19 (12 percent) were in Group B(2), 71 (45 percent) in Group C(3), and 69 (43 percent) in Group D(4). Of the 19 in Group B(2), 18 (95 percent) answered "not at all" and 1 (5 percent) answered "to a moderate degree." Of the 71 in Group C(3), 63 (89 percent) answered "not at all"; 1 (1 percent) had no opinion; 4 (6 percent) stated "to a small degree"; 2 (3 percent), "to a moderate degree"; and 1 (1 percent), "to a high degree." Of the 69 in Group D(4), 61 (89 percent) answered "not at all"; 1 (1 percent) had no opinion; 6 (9 percent) stated "to a small degree"; and 1 (1 percent), "to a high degree."

Of the 161 answering the query regarding a basic female need to experience bearing and rearing children, 19 (12 percent) were in Group B(2), and 71 (44 percent) in each of Groups C(3) and D(4). Of the 19 women in Group B(2), 1 (5 percent) had no opinion; 5 (26 percent) answered that there is "not at all" such a basic female need; 5 (26 percent) stated "to a small degree"; 5 (26 percent), "to a moderate degree"; and 3 (16 percent), "to a high degree." Of the 71 in Group C(3), one (1 percent) had no opinion; 32 (45 percent) answered "not at all"; 10 (14 percent), "to a small degree"; 16 (23 percent), "to a moderate degree"; 8 (11 percent), "to a high degree"; and 4 (6 percent), "very definitely." Of the 71 responding in Group D(4), 5 women (7 percent) had no opinion; 14 (20 percent) stated "not at all"; 14 (20 percent), "to a small degree"; 23 (32 percent), "to a moderate degree"; 13 (18 percent), "to a high degree"; and 2 (3 percent), "very definitely."

Of the 158 women responding to the question, "Did you enjoy the attention being pregnant afforded?" 19 (12 percent) were in Group B(2), 70 (44 percent) in Group C(3), and 69 (44 percent) in Group D(4). Of the 19 in Group B(2), 3 (16 percent) answered "not at all"; 2 (11 percent), "to a small degree"; 7 (37 percent), "to a moderate degree"; 6 (32 percent), "to a high degree"; and 1 (5 percent), "very definitely." Of the 70 in Group C(3), 1 (1 percent) had no opinion; 14 (20 percent) answered "not at all"; 29 (41 percent), "to a small degree"; 13 (19 percent), "to a moderate degree"; 8 (11 percent), "to a high degree"; and 5 (7 percent), "very definitely." Of the 69 women in Group D(4), 2 (3 percent) had no opinion; 27 (39 percent) answered "not at all"; 23 (33 percent), "to a small degree"; 14 (20 percent), "to a moderate degree"; 1 (1 percent), "to a high degree"; and 2 (3 percent), "very definitely."

Of the 159 women replying to the query, "Did you become pregnant to please your parents?" 19 (12 percent) were in Group B(2), 71 (45 percent) in Group C(3), and 69 (43 percent) in Group D(4). All of the 19 women in Group B(2) answered "not at all." Of the 71 in Group C(3), 58 (82 percent) answered "not at all"; 1 (1 percent) had no opinion; 5 (7 percent) stated "to a small degree"; 6 (8 percent), "to a moderate degree"; and 1 (1 percent), "to a high degree." Of the 69 women responding in Group D(4), 68 (99 percent) answered "not at all." The one other woman had no opinion.

Of the 150 women responding to the query, "Did you become pregnant to please your mate?" 19 (13 percent) were in Group B(2), 67 (45 percent) in Group C(3), and 64 (42 percent) in Group D(4). Of the 19 women in Group B(2), 12 (63 percent) answered "not at all"; 4 (21 percent) stated "to a small degree"; 2 (11 percent), "to a moderate degree"; and 1 (5 percent), "very definitely." Of the 67 women in Group C(3), 44 (66 percent) answered "not at all"; 9 (13 percent) stated "to a small degree"; 9 (13 percent), "to a moderate degree"; 2 (3 percent), "to a high degree"; and 2 (3 percent), "very definitely:" Of the 64 women answering in Group D(4), 36 (56 percent) stated "not at all"; 12 (19 percent), "to a small degree"; 7 (11 percent), "to a moderate degree"; 2 (3 percent), "to a high degree"; and 4 (6 percent), "very definitely."

Attitudes Toward Influence of Government, Schools, and Churches

Table 53 indicates that respondents in the survey were fairly unanimous with respect to the statement that parents should have primary responsibility for the care, support, protection, and entertainment of their children. Over 78 percent strongly agreed and 19 percent agreed with some reservations. Of those who strongly agreed, 16 percent were in Group A(1), 27 percent in Group B(2), 29 percent in Group C(3), and 28 percent in Group D(4).

The respondents were also in fairly close agreement in their attitudes toward governmental or UN interference with individual procreation rights. Approximately 65 percent strongly disagreed with the statement that the federal government or the UN should decide how many children each person should procreate. Over 77 percent of Group D(4) strongly disagreed and 73 percent of Group C(3) did. Slightly over 50 percent of the two younger groups strongly disagreed. About 19 percent of total respondents disagreed with reservations. Only 4 percent of all groups strongly agreed with the statement.

Regarding the statement that people on welfare should be denied the right to procreate while being supported by public funds, 30 percent strongly disagreed, 30 percent disagreed with reservations, slightly over 20 percent agreed with reservations, and 16 percent strongly agreed. Agreement and disagreement were spread fairly evenly across groups, weighted a little more heavily in the older groups.

Seventy-one percent of respondents strongly disagreed that raising children would be easier if there were governmental standards to guide parents and 13 percent disagreed with reservations. Only 2 percent strongly agreed and 6 percent agreed with reservations. Percentages of negative and affirmative responses were spread evenly across groups.

As to whether government-sponsored child-care centers might constitute invasion of parental rights, 39 percent of all respondents strongly disagreed that they might, 26 percent disagreed with reservations. About the same number of people in each group strongly disagreed; however, this figure constituted 53 percent of respondents in Group A(1), 40 percent of Group B(2), 39 percent of Group C(3), and 29 percent of Group D(4). Of those strongly agreeing that goverment child-care centers would constitute invasion of rights, 42 percent were in Group D(4) and 27 percent in Group C(3).

Sixty-six percent of respondents strongly disagreed that public schools constitute a threat to parents' rights and 20 percent disagreed with reservations. The percentages across groups were fairly equal. Only 4 percent strongly agreed that public schools do constitute such a threat.

Parental Evaluation of Support Offered by Community Institutions

As Table 54 shows, there were 243 parents responding to the query concerning the supportiveness of schools. Only one parent, who found schools "indifferent," replied from Group A(1). There were 13 parents in Group B(2) responding, 6 (46 percent) of whom found schools "supportive"; one (8 percent), "contradictory"; and 6 (46 percent), "indifferent." The preponderance of respondents to this question were in Groups C(3) and D(4), with 45 percent in Group C(3) and 49 percent in Group D(4). Seventy percent of those in Group C(3) and 77 percent of those in Group D(4) found schools supportive of their values; 8 percent of each of these groups found them "contradictory." Twenty-two percent of Group C(3) and 15 percent of Group D(4) found them "indifferent."

Again, with respect to church influence, only one parent, who found church influence "indifferent," replied from Group A(1). There were 17 parents responding from Group B(2), 13 (76 percent) of whom found church influence supportive of their values and 4 (24 percent) of whom found it "indifferent."

Ninety-one of the 219 parents responding to the query concerning church influence, or 42 percent, were in Group C(3) and 110, or 50 percent, were in Group D(4). Approximately 82 percent of Group C(3) and 84 percent of Group D(4) found church influence "supportive," 4 percent of Group C(3) and 5 percent of Group D(4) found it "contradictory." Thirteen percent of Group C(3) and 12 percent of Group D(4) found it "indifferent."

As to other community institutions, a total of 142 parents responded, 42 percent of whom were in Group C(3) and 54 percent in Group D(4). All but one person in Group C(3)found these institutions "supportive."

Attitudes Toward Nuclear Family, Extended Family

As shown in Table 55, of the 519 people responding to the statement that the nuclear family, consisting only of father, mother, and children, is no longer a good environment in which to raise children, 68 percent strongly disagreed, and another 18 percent disagreed with reservations. Of those strongly disagreeing, 17 percent were in Group A(1), 28 percent in Group B(2), 31 percent in Group C(3), and 25 percent in Group D(4). Only 18 people (3 percent) strongly agreed with the statement, and 33 (6 percent) agreed with reservations.

Twelve percent of the respondents had no opinion regarding the statement that people should try to live close to kinfolk so that blood-related extended families might again become prevalent. Fifteen percent, distributed fairly evenly across age groups, strongly disagreed with the statement and 26 percent, also distributed fairly evenly across age groups, disagreed with reservations. Almost 35 percent of the respondents agreed with reservations, 64 percent of whom were in the two older groups. Sixty-four people (12 percent) strongly agreed with the statement, 66 percent of whom were also in the two older groups.

Thirty percent of the respondents had no opinion as to the need for devising some kind of contemporary extended family that would include non-kinfolk, even neighborhood strangers. Twenty-three percent of the respondents strongly disagreed with the idea, 68 percent of whom were in Groups C(3) and D(4). About 17 percent of the respondents disagreed with reservations, 56 percent of whom were in the two older groups. Those who agreed with reservations were 24 percent of all respondents, comprising 16 percent of Group A(1), 29 percent of Group B(2), 33 percent of Group C(3), and 22 percent of Group D(4). Only 31 people (6 percent) strongly agreed with the idea of non-kin extended families, 32 percent of whom were in Group A(1), 26 percent in Group B(2), 19 percent in Group C(3), and 23 percent in Group D(4).

Thirty-six percent of the respondents had no opinion about the statement that "Intentional extended families without patriarchs can be made to work." Thirteen percent strongly disagreed and 9 percent disagreed with reservations. Twenty-seven percent agreed with reservations, 54 percent of whom were in Groups C(3) and D(4). Seventy-eight people (15 percent) strongly agreed with the possibility of making nonpatriarchal, extended families work, 63 percent of whom were in Groups A(1) and B(2).

TABLE 23: ASPIRATIONS AND GOALS

Group A(1):(Age 25 and Under)

	Have No Opinion	Of No Importance	Not Very Important	Somewhat Important	Highly Important	Most Important	Total Responses (Out of 95)
Making a happy life for myself				1	29	64	94
Having interesting work to do			1	7	56	30	94
Building myself a finan- cially secure future			6	46	32	10	94
Having a satisfactory sex life	1		2	25	49	17	94
Having a happy family life		2	5	9	36	41	93
Having grandchildren in my old age	3	24	43	20	2	1	93
Having children to carry on the family name	3	36	36	14	4		93
Having children who will carry on my ideas and values	1	26	25	27	10	2	91
Providing a better future for my children	5	9	7	25	40	6	92
Raising children to be self-respecting citizens	2	9	7	25	30	18	91
Raising happy, healthy children	2	8	5	7	31	39	92
Raising creative children who will likely be non- conformist	5	16	12	28	21	10	92
Assuring my children a college education	4	8	8	34	27	11	92

TABLE 23: (continued)

Group A(1) (Age 25 and under)	Have No Opinion	Of No Importance	Not Very Important	Somewhat Important	Highly Important	Most Important	Total Responses (Out of 95)
Continuing my own education	1	1	1	27	46	18	94
Having time and freedom to express and develop my own talents			1	11	40	42	94
Improving myself spiritually	5	10	19	27	16	15	92
Establishing for myself a respected place in my community		12	30	39	12	1	94
Attaining a position of influence and power	2	30	36	16	8	2	94
Helping make my neighborhood a decent, friendly place	1	2	15	54	20	2	94
Lending a hand to people in need in my neighborhood	6	1	6	51	20	10	94
Lending a hand to people in need in my community	6	1	6	50	21	10	94
Lending a hand to people in need in the nation	5	4	13	42	24	5	93
Lending a hand to people in need in the world	5	7	13	45	15	8	93
Working with other people to bring brotherhood to the world	7	4	14	33	22	9	89
Other (e.g.: Trying to save what remains of nature; Maintaining individual freedoms.)					2	4	6

TABLE 24:   ASPIRATIONS AND GOALS

Group B(2):   (Age 26 to 31, incl.)

	Have No Opinion	Of No Importance	Not Very Important	Somewhat Important	Highly Important	Most Important	Total Responses (Out of 139)
Making a happy life for myself			1	8	32	98	139
Having interesting work to do			1	21	78	39	139
Building myself a financially secure future	1	3	9	50	63	13	139
Having a satisfactory sex life			6	37	74	21	138
Having a happy family life	2	2	2	10	48	74	138
Having grandchildren in my old age	12	35	53	33	4		137
Having children to carry on the family name	7	59	45	24	2		137
Having children who will carry on my ideas and values	2	48	38	32	14	3	137
Providing a better future for my children	9	19	15	35	42	15	135
Raising children to be self-respecting citizens	5	15	10	35	40	32	137
Raising happy, healthy children	3	14	8	6	39	67	137
Raising creative children who will likely be non-conformist	19	27	36	28	13	11	134
Assuring my children a college education	9	16	28	41	34	9	137

TABLE 24: (continued)

Group B(2) (Age 26 to 31, incl.)	Have No Opinion	Of No Importance	Not Very Important	Somewhat Important	Highly Important	Most Important	Total Responses (Out of 139)
Continuing my own education	2	7	25	45	34	26	139
Having time and freedom to express and develop my own talents	1	2	2	21	65	48	139
Improving myself spiritually	9	17	28	35	28	22	139
Establishing for myself a respected place in my community	4	23	52	44	14	2	139
Attaining a position of influence and power	6	52	46	25	8	2	139
Helping make my neighborhood a decent, friendly place	3	9	28	55	39	5	139
Lending a hand to people in need in my neighborhood		6	17	57	46	11	137
Lending a hand to people in need in my community	1	9	25	62	33	8	138
Lending a hand to people in need in the nation	4	12	37	58	21	7	139
Lending a hand to people in need in the world	7	13	37	55	19	8	139
Working with other people to bring brotherhood to the world	6	17	35	41	23	14	136
Other (e.g.: Making a good marriage; Developing and maintaining friendships; Making other people happy; Taking responsibility for my own life; Making government fiscally responsible.)					6	9	15

TABLE 25:   ASPIRATIONS AND GOALS

Group C(3):   (Age 32 to 44, incl.)

	Have No Opinion	Of No Importance	Not Very Important	Somewhat Important	Highly Important	Most Important	Total Responses (Out of 152)
Making a happy life for myself				15	54	80	149
Having interesting work to do			2	33	75	41	151
Building myself a financially secure future		2	7	74	54	14	151
Having a satisfactory sex life		1	11	68	59	12	151
Having a happy family life			3	9	50	90	152
Having grandchildren in my old age	9	38	46	45	9	3	150
Having children to carry on the family name	6	75	42	21	6		150
Having children who will carry on my ideas and values	3	43	36	43	19	5	149
Providing a better future for my children	4	15	12	45	48	26	150
Raising children to be self-respecting citizens	1	14	1	16	60	59	151
Raising happy, healthy children	1	11		6	34	98	150
Raising creative children who will likely be non-conformist	11	32	43	35	18	8	147
Assuring my children a college education	2	15	21	55	39	16	148

TABLE 25: (continued)

Group C(3) (Age 32 to 44, incl.)	Have No Opinion	Of No Importance	Not Very Important	Somewhat Important	Highly Important	Most Important	Total Responses (Out of 152)
Continuing my own education	2	18	22	67	27	12	148
Having time and freedom to express and develop my own talents		1	71	48	65	29	150
Improving myself spiritually	8	24	27	50	27	15	151
Establishing for myself a respected place in my community	1	19	56	56	16	1	149
Attaining a position of influence and power	1	59	54	26	7	1	148
Helping make my neighborhood a decent, friendly place		6	21	72	41	9	149
Lending a hand to people in need in my neighborhood	1	7	19	72	42	10	151
Lending a hand to people in need in my community	2	6	24	81	34	3	150
Lending a hand to people in need in the nation	5	11	46	65	22	2	151
Lending a hand to people in need in the world	8	12	47	61	21	2	151
Working with other people to bring brotherhood to the world	7	19	41	50	26	4	147
Other (e.g.: Assuring existence of a viable world; Making sure parents have comfortable retirement; Realizing my full potential; Having close friends.)	1				2	7	10

TABLE 26:   ASPIRATIONS AND GOALS

Group D(4):   (Age 45 and Over)

	Have No Opinion	Of No Importance	Not Very Important	Somewhat Important	Highly Important	Most Important	Total Responses (Out of 139)
Making a happy life for myself			2	22	56	56	136
Having interesting work to do			1	22	83	30	136
Building myself a financially secure future		1	8	45	48	31	133
Having a satisfactory sex life	6	5	15	49	42	16	133
Having a happy family life	3	3	4	5	45	79	139
Having grandchildren in my old age	10	22	28	42	26	9	137
Having children to carry on the family name	7	50	38	25	10	2	132
Having children who will carry on my ideas and values	6	23	36	45	17	6	133
Providing a better future for my children	5	10	12	37	40	27	131
Raising children to be self-respecting citizens	4	6		3	31	88	132
Raising happy, healthy children	3	8		4	25	92	132
Raising creative children who will likely be non-conformist	14	24	34	33	13	11	129
Assuring my children a college education	7	11	13	38	38	25	132

TABLE 26: (continued)

Group D(4) (Age 45 and Over)	Have No Opinion	Of No Importance	Not Very Important	Somewhat Important	Highly Important	Most Important	Total Responses (Out of 139)
Continuing my own education	2	16	36	38	29	13	134
Having time and freedom to express and develop my own talents	2	3	7	41	58	26	137
Improving myself spiritually	5	16	24	37	30	25	137
Establishing for myself a respected place in my community	3	9	30	59	22	12	135
Attaining a position of influence and power	2	69	43	16	4	2	136
Helping make my neighborhood a decent, friendly place	1	4	7	61	49	13	135
Lending a hand to people in need in my neighborhood	2		8	52	47	21	130
Lending a hand to people in need in my community	2	2	12	59	44	13	132
Lending a hand to people in need in the nation	5	6	22	65	23	11	132
Lending a hand to people in need in the world	8	10	28	60	18	9	133
Working with other people to bring brotherhood to the world	16	12	17	48	28	10	131
Other (e.g.: Attaining rapport with Oversoul and life force; Avoiding government interference; Preserving an ecological balance in nature; Retiring and writing about what has been in my head for years.)				1	3	9	13

TABLE 27: COMPARATIVE RESPONSES TO FOUR CATEGORIES OF ASPIRATIONS AND GOALS

(In percentages showing affirmative responses to two opposing sets of combined choices: "Of no importance/Not very important" and "Highly important/Most important.")

Aspirations and Goals That Are Self-serving:

	Of no importance/Not very important				Highly important/Most important			
	A(1)	B(2)	C(3)	D(4)	A(1)	B(2)	C(3)	D(4)
Making a happy life for myself		0.7		1.5	99.0	93.5	89.9	82.4
Having interesting work to do	1.1	0.7	1.3	0.7	91.5	84.2	76.9	83.1
Building myself a financially secure future	6.4	8.7	5.9	6.8	44.6	54.7	45.1	59.4
Having a satisfactory sex life	2.1	4.3	8.0	15.1	70.2	68.8	47.0	43.6
Having grandchildren in my old age	72.0	64.2	56.0	36.5	3.3	2.9	8.0	25.6
Having children to carry on my ideas and values	56.1	62.7	53.1	44.4	13.2	12.4	16.2	17.3

TABLE 27 (continued)

Aspirations and Goals That Are Self-serving: (continued)

	Of no importance/Not very important				Highly important/Most important			
	A(1)	B(2)	C(3)	D(4)	A(1)	B(2)	C(3)	D(4)
Continuing my own education	2.2	23.0	26.9	38.8	68.0	43.2	26.2	31.3
Having time and freedom to express and develop my own talents	1.1	2.8	5.4	7.3	87.3	81.3	62.6	61.3
Improving myself spiritually	31.6	32.3	33.8	29.2	33.7	35.9	27.8	40.1
Establishing for myself a respected place in my community	44.7	53.9	50.0	28.9	13.9	11.5	11.4	25.2
Attaining a position of influence and power	70.2	70.5	75.3	82.3	10.6	7.2	5.4	4.4

TABLE 27 (continued)

Aspirations and Goals That Serve Family:

	Of no importance/Not very important				Highly Important/Most important			
	A(1)	B(2)	C(3)	D(4)	A(1)	B(2)	C(3)	D(4)
Having a happy family life	7.6	2.8	2.0	5.1	82.8	88.4	92.1	89.2
Having children to carry on the family name	77.4	75.9	78.0	66.7	4.3	1.5	4.6	9.1

Those Directed Toward the Welfare of Children:

	Of no importance/Not very important				Highly Important/Most important			
	A(1)	B(2)	C(3)	D(4)	A(1)	B(2)	C(3)	D(4)
Providing a better future for my children	15.2	20.8	12.7	11.4	50.0	42.2	49.3	51.1
Raising happy, healthy children	14.1	16.0	7.3	6.1	76.1	77.4	88.0	88.6
Assuring my children a college education	17.4	32.1	24.3	18.1	41.3	31.4	37.2	47.7

TABLE 27 (continued)

Aspirations and Goals Serving Social Aims of Community, Nation, World:

	Of no importance/Not very important				Highly Important/Most important			
	A(1)	B(2)	C(3)	D(4)	A(1)	B(2)	C(3)	D(4)
Raising children to be self-respecting citizens	17.6	18.2	10.0	4.5	52.8	52.6	78.8	90.2
Raising children who will likely be non-conformist	30.4	47.0	50.7	45.0	33.7	17.9	17.6	18.6
Helping make my neighborhood a decent, friendly place	18.1	26.6	18.1	8.2	23.4	31.7	33.5	45.9
Lending a hand to people in need in my neighborhood	7.5	16.8	17.2	6.2	31.9	41.6	34.4	52.4
Lending a hand to people in need in my community	7.5	24.6	20.0	10.6	32.9	29.7	24.7	43.1
Lending a hand to people in need in the nation	18.3	35.2	37.8	21.2	31.2	20.1	15.9	25.7
Lending a hand to people in need in the world	21.5	36.0	39.0	28.6	24.7	19.5	15.2	20.3

TABLE 27 (continued)

Aspirations and Goals Serving Social Aims of Community, Nation, World: (continued)

	Of no importance/Not very important				Highly important/Most important			
	A(1)	B(2)	C(3)	D(4)	A(1)	B(2)	C(3)	D(4)
Working with other people to bring brotherhood to the world	20.2	38.2	40.8	22.2	34.8	27.2	20.4	29.0
Other: (e.g., trying to save what is left of nature, maintaining individual freedoms)					n=6	n=15	n=10	n=13*

(*Percentages not figured)

TABLE 28: ATTITUDES TOWARD SEXUAL PRACTICES

	Have no opinion A (1)	B (2)	C (3)	D (4)	Totals: Have no opinion	Don't use or take part in, strongly disapprove for everyone A (1)	B (2)	C (3)	D (4)	Totals: Strongly disapprove	Disapprove, don't use or take part in, but tolerate for others A (1)	B (2)	C (3)	D (4)	Totals: Tolerate for others	Approve, but don't use or take part in A (1)	B (2)	C (3)	D (4)	Totals: Approve but don't use	Disapprove, but use or take part in A (1)	B (2)	C (3)	D (4)	Totals: Disapprove but use	Approve and use or take part in A (1)	B (2)	C (3)	D (4)	Totals: Approve and use	Totals A (1)	B (2)	C (3)	D (4)
Premarital cohabitation		2	3	9	14	1	4	9	29	43	4	13	44	57	118	43	48	60	23	174	1	0	2	2	5	46	71	30	17	164	95	138	148	137
Group marriage	10	16	12	11	49	10	24	47	86	167	37	47	70	39	193	38	50	17	2	107	0	0	0	0	0	0	0	1	0	1	95	137	147	138
Homosexual cohabitation	3	6	6	15	30	6	16	34	56	112	20	47	64	44	175	64	68	42	19	193	0	0	0	1	1	2	1	2	3	8	95	138	148	138
Use of the "Pill"	0	1	4	8	13	4	5	2	12	23	10	11	12	14	47	45	60	81	79	265	3	3	3	1	10	33	59	46	17	155	95	139	148	131
Use of the I.U.D.	1	4	6	18	29	2	6	5	13	26	7	9	10	13	39	72	96	98	80	346	1	3	3	1	8	12	21	25	7	65	95	139	147	132
Use of other contraceptives*	1	2	5	13	21	1	0	0	3	4	4	4	2	10	20	58	75	93	68	294	1	0	3	1	5	30	58	41	30	159	95	138	145	125
Abortion	2	3	2	5	12	5	12	8	15	40	10	14	34	17	75	63	83	83	83	312	0	2	3	0	5	15	22	18	11	66	95	136	148	131
Vasectomy	0	1	2	5	8	1	1	1	6	9	3	4	7	6	20	83	120	103	80	386	0	0	1	0	1	8	9	34	37	88	95	135	148	134
Development of a male "Pill"	5	7	15	23	50	2	3	4	7	16	2	4	4	4	14	66	102	105	84	357	2	1	0	1	4	18	18	18	13	67	95	135	146	132

*condom, diaphragm, rhythm, etc.

TABLE 29 : ATTITUDES TOWARD NEED, DESIRABILITY, RESPONSIBILITY OF PARENTHOOD

	Have no opinion				Totals: Have no opinion	Strongly disagree				Totals: Strongly disagree	Disagree with reservations				Total: Disagree with reservations	Agree with reservations				Totals: Agree with reservations	Strongly agree				Totals: Strongly agree	Totals			
	A (1)	B (2)	C (3)	D (4)		A (1)	B (2)	C (3)	D (4)		A (1)	B (2)	C (3)	D (4)		A (1)	B (2)	C (3)	D (4)		A (1)	B (2)	C (3)	D (4)		A (1)	B (2)	C (3)	D (4)
Satisfactions of parenthood outweigh sacrifices	6	13	6	7	32	5	1	5	3	14	12	16	5	1	34	37	61	48	32	178	33	48	86	94	261	93	139	150	137
Childless married couples are usually frustrated and unhappy	7	8	19	28	62	59	87	85	43	274	20	35	35	44	134	7	5	10	18	40	1	3	3	5	12	94	138	152	138
Children are chief source of meaning and purpose in life	1	3	2	6	12	65	83	63	29	240	18	36	42	33	129	9	12	37	45	103	1	5	8	22	36	94	139	152	135
The coming of children improves marital relationships	7	10	16	15	48	42	69	61	39	211	28	32	43	40	143	13	23	27	32	95	3	5	3	12	23	93	139	150	138
A child is part of a divine plan	18	31	27	21	97	51	75	73	38	237	12	9	8	17	46	6	10	26	27	69	8	14	17	32	71	95	139	151	135
Producing a child proves that a person is sexually mature	2	4	3	9	18	86	120	134	108	448	3	2	2	10	17	2	9	4	4	19	1	3	7	7	18	94	138	150	138
People should leave to chance or Providence, the having or not having of children	1	2	1	6	10	83	125	136	107	451	6	8	8	19	41	0	1	4	4	9	5	3	3	3	14	95	139	152	139
Married couples should have the right to choose whether or not to have children and the number	0	0	2	1	3	4	6	6	4	20	6	11	3	3	23	16	19	22	20	77	69	103	119	109	400	95	139	152	137
Parents should be able to get a legal "divorce" from unmanageable children	11	31	31	15	88	43	61	68	63	235	17	21	26	20	84	21	20	21	27	89	2	4	6	11	23	94	137	152	136

TABLE 30: ATTITUDES ON FAMILY DECISIONS AND DISAGREEMENTS

	Have no opinion				Totals: Have no opinion	Strongly disagree				Totals: Strongly disagree	Disagree with reservations				Totals: Disagree with reservations	Agree with reservations				Totals: Agree with reservations	Strongly agree				Totals: Strongly agree	Totals			
	A (1)	B (2)	C (3)	D (4)		A (1)	B (2)	C (3)	D (4)		A (1)	B (2)	C (3)	D (4)		A (1)	B (2)	C (3)	D (4)		A (1)	B (2)	C (3)	D (4)		A (1)	B (2)	C (3)	D (4)
Family decisions should be arrived at democratically, with each member, including children as young as 4 years, having equal vote	0	3	1	0	4	30	61	68	59	218	34	48	43	40	165	21	22	30	27	100	9	5	10	11	35	94	139	152	137
Family decisions should be arrived at by equal vote of only those members who are over 12 years of age	1	5	1	1	8	27	51	60	53	191	31	53	60	51	195	26	24	24	29	103	8	3	7	3	21	93	136	152	137
Both parents, sharing equally, should make all decisions concerning family life style, money, job selection, home location, schools, etc.	0	0	2	0	2	9	8	9	7	33	7	22	5	17	51	23	47	61	58	189	53	60	74	55	242	92	137	151	137
If parents can't come to agreement on family decisions, the father should have the final word	5	4	5	2	16	54	80	58	41	233	18	26	30	36	110	10	20	38	41	109	7	9	20	17	53	94	139	151	137
In serious parental disagreements involving training and discipline, the father's method should prevail	6	7	6	1	20	62	89	82	53	286	13	28	35	47	123	9	9	22	30	70	4	6	6	6	22	94	139	151	137
In serious parental disagreements involving training and discipline, the mother's way should prevail	6	6	6	1	19	56	72	71	47	246	25	37	45	65	172	5	19	27	21	72	1	5	2	2	10	93	139	151	136
If parents often can't agree regarding basic methods of training and discipline, they should call in outside counsel as soon as possible.	4	7	8	3	22	10	10	12	12	44	11	15	23	11	60	33	60	48	45	186	34	47	60	67	208	92	139	151	138

TABLE 31 : ATTITUDES TOWARD RULES FOR REARING CHILDREN

Group A(1): (under 25):

	Have no opinion	Strongly disagree	Disagree with reservations	Agree with reservations	Strongly agree	Totals (out of 95)
Punishment should not be severe but swift and certain	1	1	2	29	60	93
More time should be spent praising than showing disapproval	3		1	16	74	94
Infractions should be discussed at length with children, even with toddlers	2	10	14	32	36	94
Rules made that are reasonable should not be changed	2	29	25	30	7	93
Rules should be few and fully explained, but reasons for making them should not be given	1	66	16	5	5	93
Parental honesty is crucial. Hypocrisy cannot be hidden from children	0	2	2	15	75	94
Lecturing or warning children is a waste of breath	0	42	33	12	7	94

TABLE 31 : (continued)

Group A(1): (under 25):
(continued)

	Have no opinion	Strongly disagree	Disagree with reservations	Agree with reservations	Strongly agree	Totals (out of 95)
Compromise of rules at sub-teenage is all right but not for rules expressive of basic parental values. These should be strictly enforced regardless of contrary practice by other parents	2	11	20	36	25	94
From early age, children should within their capacity assume responsibility for their decisions and be allowed to make them	1			18	75	94
Barring destructive behavior, child should be allowed to follow his own inclinations even those not preferred by parents	1	9	7	38	39	94
Children should not be expected to show more control than parents	4	9	7	17	56	93

TABLE 32 : ATTITUDES TOWARD RULES FOR REARING CHILDREN

Group B(2): (26 to 31, incl.):

	Have no opinion	Strongly disagree	Disagree with reservations	Agree with reservations	Strongly agree	Totals (out of 139)
Punishment should not be severe but swift and certain	1	7	3	32	94	137
More time should be spent praising than showing disapproval	0	1	7	30	100	138
Infractions should be discussed at length with children, even with toddlers	1	29	27	49	31	137
Rules made that are reasonable should not be changed	4	41	38	42	13	138
Rules should be few and fully explained, but reasons for making them should not be given	2	90	30	8	5	135
Parental honesty is crucial. Hypocrisy cannot be hidden from children	1	1	2	18	117	139
Lecturing or warning children is a waste of breath	2	47	55	31	4	139

TABLE 32: (continued)

Group B(2): (26 to 31, incl.):
(continued)

	Have no opinion	Strongly disagree	Disagree with reservations	Agree with reservations	Strongly agree	Totals (out of 139)
Compromise of rules at sub-teenage is all right but not for rules expressive of basic parental values. These should be strictly enforced regardless of contrary practice by other parents	8	13	13	40	65	139
From early age, children should within their capacity assume responsibility for their decisions and be allowed to make them	2	1	2	26	108	139
Barring destructive behavior, child should be allowed to follow his own inclinations even those not preferred by parents	4	13	24	50	48	139
Children should not be expected to show more control than parents	7	12	9	33	77	138

TABLE 33: ATTITUDES TOWARD RULES FOR REARING CHILDREN

Group C(3): (32 to 44, incl.):

	Have no opinion	Strongly disagree	Disagree with reservations	Agree with Reservations	Strongly agree	Totals (out of 152)
Punishment should not be severe but swift and certain	2	3	5	44	96	150
More time should be spent praising than showing disapproval	0	0	2	33	115	150
Infractions should be discussed at length with children, even with toddlers	2	29	38	56	25	150
Rules made that are reasonable should not be changed	1	46	47	45	9	148
Rules should be few and fully explained, but reasons for making them should not be given	3	86	42	12	4	147
Parental honesty is crucial. Hypocrisy cannot be hidden from children	0	0	1	27	122	150
Lecturing or warning children is a waste of breath	2	40	61	40	7	150

TABLE 33: (continued)

Group C(3): (32 to 44, incl.):
(continued)

	Have no opinion	Strongly disagree	Disagree with reservations	Agree with Reservations	Strongly agree	Totals (out of 152)
Compromise of rules at sub-teenage is all right but not for rules expressive of basic parental values. These should be strictly enforced regardless of contrary practice by other parents	4	7	19	33	86	149
From early age, children should within their capacity assume responsibility for their decisions and be allowed to make them	3	0	1	35	110	149
Barring destructive behavior, child should be allowed to follow his own inclinations even those not preferred by parents	3	22	29	62	32	148
Children should not be expected to show more control than parents	4	7	11	42	84	148

Attitudes and Opinions of Respondents

TABLE 34: ATTITUDES TOWARD RULES FOR REARING CHILDREN

Group D(4): (45 and over):

	Totals (out of 139)	Strongly agree	Agree with reservations	Disagree with reservations	Strongly disagree	Have no opinion
Punishment should not be severe but swift and certain	138	88	40	9	1	0
More time should be spent praising than showing disapproval	139	108	27	2	2	0
Infractions should be discussed at length with children, even with toddlers	138	33	38	43	24	0
Rules made that are reasonable should not be changed	137	14	47	48	27	1
Rules should be few and fully explained, but reasons for making them should not be given	139	7	34	32	65	1
Parental honesty is crucial. Hypocrisy cannot be hidden from children	138	129	8	1	0	0
Lecturing or warning children is a waste of breath	138	8	53	52	25	0

TABLE 34: (continued)

Group D(4): (45 and over):
(continued)

	Have no opinion	Strongly disagree	Disagree with reservations	Agree with reservations	Strongly agree	Totals (out of 139)
Compromise of rules at sub-teenage is all right but not for rules expressive of basic parental values. These should be strictly enforced regardless of contrary practice by other parents	2	3	12	51	70	138
From early age, children should within their capacity assume responsibility for their decisions and be allowed to make them	1	0	1	39	96	137
Barring destructive behavior, child should be allowed to follow his own inclinations even those not preferred by parents	2	23	33	58	22	138
Children should not be expected to show more control than parents	2	5	14	34	82	137

TABLE 35:   ATTRIBUTES VALUABLE FOR A CHILD TO DEVELOP

Group A(1)   (Age 25 and under):

	Have no opinion	Of no value	Not very valuable	Somewhat valuable	Very valuable	Indispensable	Total responses (out of 95)
Self sufficiency	1	1		8	37	46	93
Competitiveness	1	1	8	58	16	7	91
Tolerance	1		1	8	49	34	93
Sociability	1		1	33	42	16	93
Loyalty	2	1	8	39	29	12	91
Detachment	10	9	29	31	9	3	91
Toughness	2	2	33	41	11	3	92
Impassiveness	8	16	40	16	8	1	89
Gentleness	2		5	22	43	20	92
Cooperation	1			10	43	39	93
Perseverance	1			17	45	30	93
Shrewdness	2	3	30	38	13	6	92
Adaptability	1			8	44	40	93
Consistency	4	2	6	29	37	14	92
Assertiveness	1		3	34	42	13	93
Candor	4		7	31	37	13	92
Good Self Image	1			4	26	62	93
Compassion	1		3	7	39	43	93
Other (e.g. in-					4	6	10

tegrity, sense of humor, imagination, understanding, love, philosophic
conviction, optimism, honesty, courtesy, awareness)

TABLE 36: ATTRIBUTES VALUABLE FOR A CHILD TO DEVELOP

Group B(2) (26 to 31, inc.):

	Have no opinion	Of no value	Not very valuable	Somewhat valuable	Very valuable	Indispensable	Total responses (out of 139)
Self sufficiency	1			6	54	77	138
Competitiveness	1	3	15	83	35	1	138
Tolerance			1	16	74	47	138
Sociability			2	39	85	12	138
Loyalty	3	1	12	52	52	18	138
Detachment	7	16	45	57	9	2	136
Toughness	2	15	34	68	16	1	136
Impassiveness	12	42	53	23	2		132
Gentleness			4	42	72	20	138
Cooperation			1	15	70	52	138
Perseverance				16	67	55	138
Shrewdness	2	7	25	73	28	2	137
Adaptability			2	11	61	64	138
Consistency		1	12	57	52	16	138
Assertiveness	1		7	56	61	13	138
Candor	2	1	7	65	55	7	137
Good Self Image		1		7	28	102	138
Compassion	1	1	2	20	61	53	138
Other (e.g. in-					5	10	15

tegrity, sense of humor, imagination, understanding, love, philosophic
conviction, optimism, honesty, courtesy, awareness)

TABLE 37: ATTRIBUTES VALUABLE FOR A CHILD TO DEVELOP

.Group C(3)   (32 to 44, inc.):

	Have no opinion	Of no value	Not very valuable	Somewhat valuable	Very valuable	Indispensable	Total responses (out of 152)
Self sufficiency	1			6	60	83	150
Competitiveness	1	3	8	79	51	7	149
Tolerance			1	23	73	54	151
Sociability			5	54	72	20	151
Loyalty	1		6	50	63	30	150
Detachment	9	24	57	43	13	1	147
Toughness	4	9	33	77	21	4	148
Impassiveness	12	47	67	15	5	1	147
Gentleness		2	9	46	73	20	150
Cooperation			2	20	75	54	151
Perseverance	1			14	80	56	151
Shrewdness	2	14	32	66	28	7	149
Adaptability				22	66	63	151
Consistency	2	1	12	48	65	23	151
Assertiveness	1	2	5	59	65	19	151
Candor	1	3	11	61	54	21	151
Good Self Image		1		5	30	115	151
Compassion		3	2	23	68	54	150
Other (e.g. in-	2				6	14	22

tegrity, sense of humor, imagination, understanding, love, philosophic
conviction, optimism, honesty, courtesy, awareness)

TABLE 38: ATTRIBUTES VALUABLE FOR A CHILD TO DEVELOP

Group D(4) (45 and over):

	Have no opinion	Of no value	Not very valuable	Somewhat valuable	Very valuable	Indispensable	Total responses (out of 139)
Self sufficiency				4	60	71	135
Competitiveness		1	12	71	43	9	136
Tolerance				10	78	48	136
Sociability			4	42	71	20	137
Loyalty	2		1	26	65	43	137
Detachment	10	18	41	49	11	5	134
Toughness	5	7	45	57	18	3	135
Impassiveness	8	40	55	22	5		130
Gentleness		1	5	34	71	23	134
Cooperation			1	14	77	44	136
Perseverance			1	13	70	53	137
Shrewdness	1	9	32	68	21	6	137
Adaptability				16	68	53	137
Consistency	1		1	27	71	37	137
Assertiveness			7	53	61	14	135
Candor	2		7	63	45	15	132
Good Self Image			2	7	45	82	136
Compassion			4	17	56	60	137
Other (e.g. in-					2	10	12

tegrity, sense of humor, imagination, understanding, love, philosophic
conviction, optimism, honesty, courtesy, awareness)

TABLE 39: COMPARATIVE GROUP CHOICES OF CHILD ATTRIBUTES
CONSIDERED MOST VALUABLE/INDISPENSABLE (In percentages)

	A(1)	B(2)	C(3)	D(4)
Self Sufficiency	89.3	94.9	95.3	97.0
Tolerance	89.3	87.7	84.1	92.7
Sociability	62.4	70.3	60.9	66.4
Loyalty	45.1	50.7	62.0	78.8
Gentleness	68.4	66.7	62.0	70.2
Cooperation*	88.1	88.4	85.5	89.0
Perseverance	80.7	88.5	90.1	89.8
Adaptability	90.3	90.6	85.4	88.3
Consistency	55.4	49.3	58.2	78.8
Assertiveness	59.2	53.6	55.6	55.6
Candor	54.3	45.2	49.7	45.5
Good Self Image	94.7	94.2	96.1	93.6
Compassion	88.1	82.6	81.3	84.7
*Compare: Competitiveness	25.3	26.1	38.9	38.2

TABLE 40: FACTORS IMPORTANT TO CHILDREN'S SELF IMAGES

	Have no opinion				Totals: Have no opinion	Strongly disagree				Totals: Strongly disagree	Disagree with reservations				Totals: Disagree with reservations	Agree with reservations				Totals: Agree with reservations	Strongly agree				Totals: Strongly agree	Totals			
	A (1)	B (2)	C (3)	D (4)		A (1)	B (2)	C (3)	D (4)		A (1)	B (2)	C (3)	D (4)		A (1)	B (2)	C (3)	D (4)		A (1)	B (2)	C (3)	D (4)		A (1)	B (2)	C (3)	D (4)
Most important is what children think their parents think of them	7	7	9	0	23	16	11	10	16	53	10	13	21	19	63	32	52	58	50	192	27	56	50	52	185	92	139	148	137
Most important is what children think their peers think of them	5	7	7	2	21	12	12	7	10	41	9	9	14	5	37	39	61	59	54	213	28	50	61	67	204	93	139	148	138

TABLE 41: REASONS PARENTS HAD FIRST CHILD

	Group A(1)	Group B(2)	Group C(3)	Group D(4)	Totals
It happened accidentally	0	6	20	17	43
I thought that's what was expected in marriage	0	0	4	5	9
I wanted something of my very own to take care of and have the say about	0	1	3	5	9
I wanted to give someone else the happy childhood I never had	0	0	1	0	1
I felt my marriage would be more complete with a child	1	4	22	31	58
I wanted to please my mate	0	0	2	5	7
I thought a child would save my faltering marriage	0	0	0	0	0
Because of religious convictions	0	0	0	0	0
Other reasons (see pp. 84-86)	0	17	45	37	99
Multiple reasons (see pp. 86-88)	0	5	24	19	48 $\overline{274}$

TABLE 42: REASONS PARENTS HAD SECOND CHILD

	Group B(2)	Group C(3)	Group D(4)	Totals
It happened accidentally	2	11	12	25
I thought that's what was expected in marriage	0	1	2	3
I wanted my child to have brother(s), sister(s)	1	47	65	113
I wanted to give more than one child the happy childhood I never had	0	2	0	2
I felt my marriage would be more complete with an expanded family	1	7	9	17
I wanted to please my mate	0	2	1	3
I thought another child would save my faltering marriage	0	2	0	2
I thought another child would keep me young	0	0	0	0
Because of religious convictions	0	1	0	1
Other reasons (see pp. 88-89)	2	4	11	17
Multiple reasons (see pp. 88-89)	2	13	13	28
				211

TABLE 43:   MOST FREQUENTLY STATED REASONS DETERRING RESPONDENTS
FROM HAVING FIRST CHILD, SUBSEQUENT CHILDREN

	A(1)	B(2)	C(3)	D(4)	Totals
First Child:					
High cost	0	2	2	3	7
Overpopulation	0	1	1	0	2
Other (e.g., lack of time, selfish motives, don't want the responsibility	2	1	6	3	12
Second Child:					
High cost	0	2	5	2	9
Overpopulation	0	1	2	2	5
Other (e.g., unstable family conditions, inability to cope, medical reasons)	0	3	7	3	13
Third Child:					
High cost	0	4	8	6	18
Overpopulation	0	3	12	3	18
Other (e.g., husband doesn't want more children, lack of energy, lack of money)	0	1	10	7	18
Fourth Child:					
High cost	0	1	6	4	11
Overpopulation	0	3	5	3	11
Other (e.g., age, physical disability)	0	1	5	8	14

TABLE 44 : PARENTAL OPINIONS CONCERNING CHILDREN AS HINDRANCES

	Have no opinion (1) A	(2) B	(3) C	(4) D	Totals: Have no opinion	Not at all (1) A	(2) B	(3) C	(4) D	Totals: Not at all	To a small degree (1) A	(2) B	(3) C	(4) D	Totals: To a small degree	To a moderate degree (1) A	(2) B	(3) C	(4) D	Totals: To a moderate degree	To a high degree (1) A	(2) B	(3) C	(4) D	Totals: To a high degree	Very definitely (1) A	(2) B	(3) C	(4) D	Totals: Very definitely	Totals (1) A	(2) B	(3) C	(4) D
Is (was) your child (children) a hindrance to you in job selection?	1	0	1	4	6	1	22	65	70	158	0	1	14	10	25	0	1	13	8	22	0	2	7	3	12	0	2	6	4	12	2	28	106	99
A hindrance to you in travel opportunities?	1	0	2	2	5	1	5	20	41	67	0	9	28	28	65	0	6	28	20	54	0	5	20	12	37	0	4	10	3	17	2	29	108	106
A hindrance to you in general mobility?	2	0	2	1	5	0	2	30	50	82	1	9	21	30	61	0	11	33	14	58	0	4	16	6	26	0	3	10	2	15	3	29	112	103
A hindrance to you in saving money?	1	1	1	0	3	0	3	30	21	54	1	11	28	28	68	0	6	28	31	65	0	5	12	21	38	0	4	11	10	25	2	30	110	111
A hindrance to you in staying out of debt?	1	2	2	3	8	1	16	58	46	121	0	6	17	27	50	0	4	16	14	34	0	1	6	7	14	0	1	4	8	13	2	30	103	105
A hindrance to you in having free time for personal pursuits?	1	0	2	0	3	0	3	8	25	36	1	5	31	35	72	0	10	30	29	69	0	8	27	12	47	0	3	16	5	24	2	29	114	106

TABLE 45: PERCENTAGE OF DISAGREEMENTS
            BETWEEN SPOUSES, COHABITANTS
            OR OTHER ADULTS IN HOME OVER
            CHILDREN OF THE HOUSEHOLD

	A(1)	B(2)	C(3)	D(4)	Totals
Zero percent	1	10	22	27	60
10 percent	1	11	56	50	118
20 percent	0	5	22	19	46
50 percent	2	3	14	12	31
Over 50 percent	1	1	3	8	13

TABLE 46 : CAUSES OF DISAGREEMENTS OVER CHILDREN

	A(1)	B(2)	C(3)	D(4)	Totals
Differences regarding child's (children's) behavioral training	2	17	61	52	132
Differences regarding child's (children's) religious training	0	0	7	4	11
Differences as to methods of correction	3	11	68	46	128
Differences as to which adult should have final say about punishment	1	1	7	7	16
Differences about behavior of step-children	0	0	1	3	4
School troubles	1	1	2	13	17
Trouble with neighbors	0	0	5	10	15
Feelings of incapacity to cope with recalci-trant children	1	0	14	8	23
Money difficulties involving costs of raising children	0	2	9	14	25

TABLE 47: ATTITUDES TOWARD INFLUENCE OF CHILDREN ON DIVORCE DECISIONS

	Have no opinion				Totals: Have no opinion	Not at all				Totals: Not at all	To a small degree				Totals: To a small degree	To a moderate degree				Totals: To a moderate degree	To a high degree				Totals: To a high degree	Very definitely				Totals: Very definitely	Totals			
	A (1)	B (2)	C (3)	D (4)		A (1)	B (2)	C (3)	D (4)		A (1)	B (2)	C (3)	D (4)		A (1)	B (2)	C (3)	D (4)		A (1)	B (2)	C (3)	D (4)		A (1)	B (2)	C (3)	D (4)		A (1)	B (2)	C (3)	D (4)
If divorced, do you consider your own offspring/step-offspring/adopted offspring a basic source of conflict leading up to divorce?	4	4	18	14	40	0	3	3	21	32	0	2	4	1	7	0	0	2	1	3	0	0	2	0	2	0	0	0	2	2	4	9	34	39
If divorced, would you have had the divorce had there been no children in your family?	4	4	16	14	38	0	0	1	6	7	0	0	1	1	2	0	1	1	0	2	0	2	3	7	12	0	2	11	11	24	4	9	33	39
If now married/separated and have had thoughts of divorcing does a child/children stand in your way?	4	5	16	13	38	0	5	16	21	42	0	0	7	3	10	0	0	10	2	12	0	1	9	4	14	0	4	12	4	20	4	15	70	47

TABLE 48: SOME FACTORS INDICATING DEGREE
OF PARENTAL ATTENTIVENESS

Groups B(2), C(3), D(4)

	B(2)	C(3)	D(4)	Totals
More than one hour per day spent by respondent playing or conversing with child (children)	25	82	82	189
Grandparents used as babysitters	5	8	26	39
Paid outsiders used as babysitters	10	50	40	100
Combination of grandparents, other relatives, friends, paid outsiders used as babysitters	9	36	37	82
Television used as babysitter less than 1 hour per day	16	34	40	90
Television used as babysitter 1 hour per day	6	36	27	69
Television used as babysitter 2 hours per day	1	37	23	61
Child (children) under 15 regularly ate dinner with respondent	24	111	115	250
Child (children) under 15 had regular, specific chores to do	13	99	112	224

Question	Have no opinion A (1)	B (2)	C (3)	D (4)	Totals: Have no opinion	Not at all A (1)	B (2)	C (3)	D (4)	Totals: Not at all	To a small degree A (1)	B (2)	C (3)	D (4)	Totals: To a small degree	To a moderate degree A (1)	B (2)	C (3)	D (4)	Totals: To a moderate degree	To a high degree A (1)	B (2)	C (3)	D (4)	Totals: To a high degree	Very definitely A (1)	B (2)	C (3)	D (4)	Totals: Very definitely	Totals A (1)	B (2)	C (3)	D (4)
Does (did) it comfort you to talk to someone about troubles you have (had) with your offspring?	4	4	9	5	22	0	5	7	10	22	0	1	18	29	48	0	8	22	40	70	0	4	25	12	41	0	7	35	15	57	4	29	116	111
Do (did) you take satisfaction in having an obedient child (children)?	3	5	2	1	11	1	0	1	1	3	0	4	7	14	25	1	7	35	43	86	0	11	41	37	89	0	6	37	20	63	5	33	123	116
Do you take personal satisfaction in being told your child (children) is (are) attractive, talented or well-mannered?	2	2	1	1	6	1	0	0	0	1	0	2	4	5	11	0	8	22	31	61	0	12	42	41	95	1	9	53	38	101	4	33	122	116
Does it give you pleasure to be known as someone's mother or father?	2	2	3	2	9	1	1	5	1	8	0	6	7	8	21	0	7	30	29	66	1	9	33	32	75	0	9	45	47	101	4	34	123	119
Do you feel personally triumphant in your offspring's accomplishments?	2	3	2	1	8	1	4	5	5	15	0	9	23	21	53	1	11	36	46	94	0	2	30	23	55	0	4	25	23	52	4	33	121	119
Do you think of your child (children) as an interesting project(s) to direct?	3	3	2	5	13	0	14	53	62	129	0	4	22	15	41	1	9	21	18	49	0	2	17	10	29	0	2	6	6	14	4	34	121	116

TABLE 49: (continued)

	Have no opinion				Totals: Have no opinion	Not at all				Totals: Not at all	To a small degree				Totals: To a small degree	To a moderate degree				Totals: To a moderate degree	To a high degree				Totals: To a high degree	Very definitely				Totals: Very definitely	Totals			
	A(1)	B(2)	C(3)	D(4)		A(1)	B(2)	C(3)	D(4)		A(1)	B(2)	C(3)	D(4)		A(1)	B(2)	C(3)	D(4)		A(1)	B(2)	C(3)	D(4)		A(1)	B(2)	C(3)	D(4)		A(1)	B(2)	C(3)	D(4)
Do you feel that successful children add to one's status in the community or among friends?	1	3	5	3	12	1	5	29	17	52	2	8	40	38	88	3	12	25	30	70	2	5	15	18	40	0	3	8	13	24	9	36	122	119
Do you feel you would be missing something important to your personal development if you didn't have at least one child?	1	1	1	3	6	1	4	13	11	29	0	0	14	3	17	2	8	11	12	33	2	5	18	22	47	0	20	66	69	155	6	38	123	120
Do you believe people should sacrifice for their children?	1	0	0	1	2	0	3	3	5	11	0	7	19	12	38	3	16	54	60	133	2	5	24	20	51	2	6	21	21	50	3	37	121	119
When your child (children) is (was) grossly disobedient, do (did) you take it as an affront to your right as a parent?	2	1	3	0	6	0	11	40	39	90	0	2	16	12	30	0	4	11	9	24	0	1	7	10	18	0	0	2	2	4	2	19	79	72
When your child (children) is (was) grossly disobedient, do (did) you take it as a sign of your failure as a parent?	2	1	5	0	8	0	8	31	29	68	0	3	15	24	42	0	4	20	20	44	0	2	11	16	29	0	2	4	3	9	2	20	86	92

TABLE 50: RESPONSES TO QUESTION: IF YOU
HAD IT TO DO OVER AGAIN

	A(1)	B(2)	C(3)	D(4)	Totals
I would not have any children	0	1	8	3	12
I would have only one child	0	1	4	0	5
I would have only two children	1	0	19	23	43
I'd have the number I do have	0	24	69	77	170
I'd have as many as came	0	0	8	5	13
I am undecided	0	7	13	12	32
					275

TABLE 51: PARENTAL EXPECTATIONS WITH RESPECT
TO THEIR DEPENDENCE ON CHILDREN IN
OLD AGE

	A(1) Yes	No	B(2) Yes	No	C(3) Yes	No	D(4) Yes	No	Totals Yes	No
Do you expect your child (children) to remain close to you when you are old?	2	2	24	9	85	33	76	41	187	85
Do you depend on their taking care of you when you are old?	1	3	1	32	7	115	5	115	14	265

TABLE 52 : ATTITUDES OF FEMALE PARENTS TOWARD CHILDBEARING

	Have no opinion				Totals: Have no opinion	Not at all				Totals: Not at all	To a small degree				Totals: To a small degree	To a moderate degree				Totals: To a moderate degree	To a high degree				Totals: To a high degree	Very definitely				Totals: Very definitely	Totals			
	A (1)	B (2)	C (3)	D (4)		A (1)	B (2)	C (3)	D (4)		A (1)	B (2)	C (3)	D (4)		A (1)	B (2)	C (3)	D (4)		A (1)	B (2)	C (3)	D (4)		A (1)	B (2)	C (3)	D (4)		A (1)	B (2)	C (3)	D (4)
Is (was) your desire to have a child (children) prompted by wanting "something to do"?	0	0	0	0	0	0	14	65	63	142	0	2	5	4	11	0	1	1	2	4	0	1	2	1	4	0	0	1	0	1	0	18	74	70
Was pregnancy your "finest hour"?	0	0	3	0	3	0	5	34	31	70	0	5	16	15	36	0	7	4	14	25	0	2	10	8	20	0	0	4	2	6	0	19	71	70
Do (did) you feel that emotionally you "need" (needed) to be pregnant every so often?	0	0	1	1	2	0	18	63	61	142	0	0	4	6	10	0	1	2	0	3	0	0	1	1	2	0	0	0	0	0	0	19	71	69
Do you think there is a basic female need to experience having and rearing children?	0	1	1	5	7	0	5	32	14	51	0	5	10	14	29	0	5	16	23	44	0	3	8	13	24	0	0	4	2	6	0	19	71	71
Did you enjoy the attention being pregnant afforded?	0	0	1	2	3	0	3	14	27	44	0	2	29	23	54	0	7	13	14	34	0	6	8	1	15	0	1	5	2	8	0	19	70	69
Did you become pregnant to please your parents?	0	0	1	1	2	0	19	58	68	145	0	0	5	0	5	0	0	6	0	6	0	0	1	0	1	0	0	0	0	0	0	19	71	69
Did you become pregnant to please your mate?	0	0	1	3	4	0	12	44	36	92	0	4	99	12	115	0	2	9	7	18	0	0	2	2	4	0	1	2	4	7	0	19	67	64

TABLE 53 : ATTITUDES TOWARD INFLUENCE OF GOVERNMENT, SCHOOLS AND CHURCHES ON PROCREATION AND CHILD REARING

	Have no opinion A(1)	B(2)	C(3)	D(4)	Totals: Have no opinion	Strongly disagree A(1)	B(2)	C(3)	D(4)	Totals: Strongly disagree	Disagree with reservations A(1)	B(2)	C(3)	D(4)	Totals: Disagree with reservations	Agree with reservations A(1)	B(2)	C(3)	D(4)	Totals: Agree with reservations	Strongly agree A(1)	B(2)	C(3)	D(4)	Totals: Strongly agree	Totals A(1)	B(2)	C(3)	D(4)
Parents should have primary responsibility for care, support, protection and entertainment of their children.	2	0	1	0	3	2	0	0	0	2	1	3	1	1	6	25	26	30	21	102	64	110	120	117	411	94	139	152	139
Federal government or U.N. should now decide how many children each person should procreate	1	4	1	1	7	49	74	111	107	341	25	34	24	16	99	13	22	14	8	57	7	5	2	6	20	95	139	152	138
People on welfare should be denied right to procreate while being supported by public funds	4	4	3	3	14	38	42	42	37	159	29	44	44	39	156	13	30	32	33	108	11	18	29	27	85	95	138	150	139
Raising children would be easier if there were official government standards or guidelines for family comportment	6	20	8	7	41	59	98	115	98	370	14	15	18	20	67	9	5	7	12	33	4	1	4	1	10	92	139	152	138
Public government sponsored child care centers would constitute invasion of parental right to rear children according to individual family preference	6	12	15	11	43	49	54	58	40	201	24	44	36	29	133	7	7	16	24	54	7	19	23	35	84	93	136	148	139
Public schools today constitute a threat to parents' rights and individual family values	2	3	5	2	12	59	86	105	94	344	21	37	23	21	102	8	7	13	14	42	3	6	6	6	21	93	139	152	137

TABLE 54: PARENTAL EVALUATION OF CHILD RAISING SUPPORT OFFERED BY SCHOOLS, CHURCH, OTHER COMMUNITY INSTITUTIONS

	A(1)	B(2)	C(3)	D(4)	Totals
Schools:					
Supportive of parental values	0	6	77	92	175
Contradictory	0	1	9	9	19
Indifferent	1	6	24	18	49
Church Influence:					
Supportive of parental values	0	13	75	92	180
Contradictory	0	0	4	5	9
Indifferent	1	4	12	13	30
Other Community Institutions:*					
Supportive	0	6	59	76	141
Indifferent	0	0	1	0	1

* e.g., YMCA, YWCA, Boys Club, Boy Scouts, Girl Scouts, Law Enforcement Agencies, Lions Club, City Recreation, City Parks and Playgrounds, 4-H Club. The preponderant "other" institution, however, was "Friends and Relatives."

TABLE 55 : ATTITUDES TOWARD NUCLEAR FAMILY, EXTENDED FAMILY

	Have no opinion				Totals: Have no opinion	Strongly disagree				Totals: Strongly disagree	Disagree with reservations				Totals: Disagree with reservations	Agree with reservations				Totals: Agree with reservations	Strongly agree				Totals: Strongly agree	Totals			
	A (1)	B (2)	C (3)	D (4)		A (1)	B (2)	C (3)	D (4)		A (1)	B (2)	C (3)	D (4)		A (1)	B (2)	C (3)	D (4)		A (1)	B (2)	C (3)	D (4)		A (1)	B (2)	C (3)	D (4)
The nuclear family is no longer a good environment in which to raise children	3	3	9	8	23	60	97	108	87	352	17	24	27	25	93	8	13	3	9	33	5	1	5	7	18	93	138	152	136
People should try to live closer to their kinfolk, so that blood-related extended families could again become prevalent family pattern	14	23	12	12	61	21	22	18	17	78	27	38	42	30	137	25	40	57	59	181	7	15	22	20	64	94	138	151	138
Some kind of contemporary extended family should be devised that would include non-blood related people, including strangers who happened to be neighbors	29	50	36	39	154	14	24	38	42	118	18	20	26	23	87	20	36	42	27	125	10	8	6	7	31	91	138	148	138
Intentional extended families without patriarchs can be made to work	28	48	58	49	183	7	12	19	29	67	10	9	12	14	45	25	41	46	30	142	20	29	15	14	78	90	139	150	136

6
Summation

As was noted in Chapter 4, the purpose for the survey was to try to determine whether or not attitudes and opinions elicited from a carefully selected sample of Americans might to some degree illuminate or have relation to general attitudes toward children and their meaning in the contemporary United States. The specific task was to try to discover from a given sample of people some of the reasons why they might or might not want children; why they might or might not value children; what egoistic, psychological, economic, or other needs might have induced those who were parents to have children; and what degree of commitment respondents might have felt to other individuals or to society to want or have children.

The response to the questionnaire, which was sent to 1,203 U.C.S.B. graduates (corrected to 1,156 by reason of postal nondelivery of 47) from four age groups, was over 45 percent. Of the 525 respondents, 58 percent were female and 42 percent male. All but two were U.S. citizens. Ethnic background was 93 percent Anglo-American. One-fourth of respondents had postgraduate degrees. Over 36 percent worked professionally in the field of education. At least 80 percent resided in California, and over half lived in cities of over 50,000 population — 69 percent in single-family homes. Over 61 percent owned their own homes. Fifty percent of the respondents were Protestant. Of the total respondents, 54 percent declared themselves to be "mildly" or "fairly" religious and approximately 32 percent, "not religious." Most were politically moderate or liberal. The 22 percent designating themselves "conservative" were found among the older groups.

Over 29 percent of respondents were single and never married, and 62 percent were currently married. Ninety-two percent of those who were under age 25, and 74 percent of those age 26 through 31, had never had children. These two younger groups constituted 45 percent of total respondents. Thirty-five percent of all respondents currently had one or more children of their own living with them, and an additional 2 percent had adoptive children living with them.

Approximately 15 percent of respondents had a combined annual family income of less than $10,000; one third had $15,000 to $24,999; and approximately another third, $25,000 to $49,999.

Thus, the sample had appreciable homogeneities of ethnic identity, education, religious and political attitudes, and general social status. The chief heterogeneity resulted from the deliberate selection of four age groupings, obtained by means of choosing representatives from four fairly widely separated college graduation periods.

Tentative Survey Conclusions

Regardless of some inconsistencies and apparent contradictions, which will be discussed later, the following conclusions can be drawn about the attitudes and opinions represented by the sample of this survey:

1. Children are wanted and are deemed important.
2. Raising happy, healthy children to become good citizens is an important goal today.
3. Satisfactions of parenthood outweigh the sacrifices and heartaches involved.
4. Given the chance of "doing it over again," most people would have the number of children they do have.
5. Children are only moderately a hindrance to personal pursuits of parents.
6. Religious considerations have minimal influence on attitudes and actions leading to parenthood.
7. Egoistic considerations (involving psychological-emotional aspects) leading to parenthood are strong.
8. Altruistic reasons for parenthood are few.
9. Consciously deliberated reasons for parenthood are often absent, especially among people who became parents several decades ago.
10. Younger women do not feel special needs to bear and rear offspring; older women do have such feelings to a moderate degree.
11. The capacity to procreate is not regarded as a sign of sexual maturity.
12. Procreation should be left to parental choice, not to chance or Divine Providence.
13. Parents should have primary responsibility for care, support, protection, and entertainment of their children; there should be no bureaucratic interference with parental rights of procreation and nurture.
14. Schools, churches, and other community institutions are regarded as supportive in the task of raising children.

15. Overpopulation is a deterrent to procreation only after the birth of a first child.
16. Money difficulties involving costs of raising children are not an appreciable cause of family disagreements, yet the high cost of raising children is an important deterrent to procreation.
17. The traditional reason of being supported in old age by children is no longer cause for procreation.
18. Carrying on the family name or parental ideas or values are now not very important reasons for having children.
19. Older people are more inclined to want to live near kinfolk than are younger people.
20. The nuclear family is still regarded as a good environment in which to raise children.
21. Older people are much less inclined than are younger ones to countenance the idea of an extended family that would include strangers.
22. Intentional family units without patriarchs are thought to be possible today.
23. Personal and immediate family goals carry more weight than broader social aims; more emphasis is placed on community and neighborhood goals than on those of the nation or world.
24. What children think their parents think of them is considered as important to children's self-images as what children think their peers think of them.
25. There is no significant lack of parental attentiveness to children.

Explication of Conclusions

In substantiation of the foregoing conclusions, I offer the following point-by-point explanations:

1. *Children are wanted and are deemed important.* Although nearly three-fourths of the respondents disagreed to some degree (over 46 percent strongly, 25 percent with reservations) that children are the chief source of meaning and purpose in life, and over half of all respondents strongly disagreed that childless married couples are usually frustrated and unhappy, all respondents rated having a happy family life as being an important aim in life.

Comparatively few respondents under age 32 answered queries in Table 49, which attempted to elicit the reflective importance of children for parents. However, of those responding in the two older groups (age 32 and over), approximately 70 percent stated they "very definitely" or "to a high degree" would be missing something important to their personal development if they did not have at least one child.

Although more than 40 percent of respondents strongly disagreed that the coming of children improves marital relationships, at least 32 percent of those age 45 and over strongly agreed, or agreed with reservations, that children *do* improve a marriage.

Perhaps the overall high percentage of negative opinions with respect to the beneficial influence of children on a marriage merely reflects recognition that the coming of children marks a common and acceptable shift of focus from marital to familial expectations, involving fulfillment through children rather than through the marital bond alone. Approximately half the parents responding found children to be the cause of only 10 percent of family disagreements, and, as shown in Table 47, respondents generally did not feel that children were a source of conflict leading to divorce, or further, that the presence of children prior to contemplation of divorce had much influence on divorce decisions.

Among explanatory remarks written by respondents, which would corroborate the conclusions that children are wanted and are important, some variation of the following often recurred: "I (we) wanted a child"; "I (we) love children"; "I have a basic desire for children."

2. *Raising happy, healthy children to become good citizens is an important goal today.* At least three-fourths of respondents stated as a goal the raising of happy, healthy children, and an interest in providing a better future for their children was indicated by at least half of all respondents.

3. *Satisfactions of parenthood outweigh the sacrifices and heartaches involved.* Over half the total respondents strongly agreed with this statement, and an additional one-third agreed with some reservations. In addition, approximately half the respondents over age 31 felt that to a moderate degree parents should sacrifice for their children. There was strong opposition (45 percent) to the suggestion that some kind of socially acceptable legal "divorce" should be made available for parents from children who have become unmanageable but not sufficiently delinquent to be made wards of a court.

4. *Given the chance of "doing it over again," most people would have the number of children they do have.* Of the 52 percent responding to the query, "If you had it to do over again, would you have children"? approximately 62 percent would have chosen to have exactly the number of children they did have. (Most of this 62 percent, of course, being over 32 years of age, had both maturity and time to have acquired experience with children.) Only 12 people (4 percent) of the 275 responding to this query would have had *no* children if they had had it to do over again.

5. *Children are only moderately a hindrance to personal pursuits of parents.* Although one-fourth of responding parents (who were between

the ages of 31 and 45) stated they felt that children were to high degree a hindrance to their having free time to follow personal goals, most felt that children were only to a small or moderate degree a hindrance to job selection, general mobility, travel opportunities, saving money, and staying out of debt.

6. *Religious considerations have minimal influence on attitudes and actions leading to parenthood.* Very few respondents, either directly in the questionnaire or in supplemental write-ins, even alluded to religious convictions as reasons for having children. In addition, although 23 percent of respondents over 45 years of age strongly agreed that a child is a part of a divine plan, over 45 percent of the total respondents strongly disagreed with this statement. The affirmative belief declared by one-fourth of the older respondents might be traced to the lingering influence of a more rigidly religious upbringing.

There were a few statements added to some of the questionnaires that could be interpreted as stemming from religious considerations, such as "That's [having children] what life is all about," or "I wanted to be part of the purpose of earth life." Over 85 percent of respondents emphatically disagreed that people should leave procreation to chance or Providence.

7. *Egoistic considerations (involving psychological-emotional aspects) leading to parenthood are strong.* From the standpoint of personal goals in life, all respondents exhibited a high degree of egocentrism. They all rated very highly having time and freedom to express and develop personal talents. Prime goals of from 80 to 90 percent of the respondents in all groups were "making a happy life for myself" and "having interesting work to do." On the other hand, the majority of respondents deemed unimportant establishing a respected place in the community or attaining power and influence.

Respondents' reasons for wanting or having children were also strongly egoistic. The write-in reasons showed considerable variation on this theme. From the more *egotistic (outwardly self-vaunting):*

My wife and I both wanted to carry on productive, intelligent people rather than allow the dullards to breed themselves into dominance.

Good genes.

We believe in ourselves and felt we should enhance society by having a child with our belief and morals.

I wanted to mold another person.

I wanted to have children to bring up and educate.

We wanted to continue the family with a "next generation."

My husband was concerned with having a "son and heir."

To the more *egoistic (inwardly self-seeking):*

I wanted the experience.

I wanted the joy a child could give.

I wanted the experience of giving birth.

I wanted the personal satisfaction of having a child.

I wanted to enjoy their personalities.

I wanted something of my very own to take care of and have the say about.

I wanted the experience of producing another life.

I didn't want *not* to have the experience.

I wanted to create a new person.

And for reasons stemming more, perhaps, from felt but not fully articulated psychological needs:

I felt an inner need for a child.

I had a really basic desire for children.

I felt an innate desire to have a family.

I had a strong maternal need.

I just wanted a child, period.

That's what life is all about.

We love children.

I just felt it would be nice to have a child.

My life would be more complete.

I felt life would be more meaningful and happy with children.

Answers to other parts of the questionnaire also had some egoistic or egocentric content. These pertained chiefly to attitudes and opinions of respondents 32 years of age and older, since replies from the two younger groups were comparatively few in these sections.

Over half of respondents age 32 through 44 and one-fourth of respondents 45 and over declared "very definitely" or "to a high degree" that they were comforted by talking over with someone the troubles they had with their offspring. Over 60 percent of those age 32 through 44, and about half of those 45 and over, took "definite" or a "high degree" of personal satisfaction in having obedient children; over three-fourths of those 32 through 44, and nearly 70 percent of those 45 and over, gained "definite" or a "high degree" of personal satisfaction from having attractive children; over 60 percent of both older groups "very definitely" or "to a high degree" liked to be known as someone's mother or father; approximately 40 percent of both older groups felt a "definite" or "high degree" of personal triumph in their children's accomplishments; and approximately 70 percent of both older groups felt "very definitely" or "to a high degree" that they would be missing something important if they were childless.

At least one-third of both older groups, to a "moderate" or a "high degree," considered gross disobedience in their children a personal failure of their own; yet an equal percentage of both groups considered such disobedience "not at all" a parental failure.

Futhermore with respect to most of the foregoing (except for the answers concerning the gross disobedience of children), from one-fourth to one-third additional respondents in the two older groups answered affirmatively as well—"to a moderate degree." Thus, if it can be stated that these answers disclose degrees of egoism, this characteristic can be said to influence reasons for procreation.

It is interesting to note here that about half the older respondents declared they felt children add to a parent's status only "to a small degree" or "not at all." This may conflict somewhat with the high affirmative percentages with respect to the statement that respondents liked to be known as someone's parent; also, it may have some relation to the more than 50 percent response of "not at all" from both older groups to the question, "Do you take it as an affront to your right as a parent when your child or children are grossly disobedient?" (It is to be noted that at least 14 percent of respondents over age 45 *did* "to a high degree" consider gross disobedience a personal affront to them, which may reflect their allegiance to traditions of earlier times.)

8. *Altruistic reasons for parenthood are few.* The following examples of responses may be considered "altruistic" reasons for having children:

I wanted to please my mate.

I wanted to give child a happy life.

I wanted to share love with a child.

I wanted my child to have brother(s), sister(s).

I felt my marriage would be more complete with more than one child. (Approximately 8 percent gave this reason.)

Some of the reasons given that were more "egotistic" (See statement 7 above) might be included here as altruistic reasons also, such as, "We believe in ourselves and felt we should enhance society by having a child with our belief and morals." About 25 percent of both older groups also gave as a reason for having children, "to complete my marriage," which, if the intent included the desire to make the marriage successful in the general society, might be said to contain an element of altruism.

The nearly unanimous negative response of women respondents to the question, "Did you get pregnant to please your mate? (your parents?)" might be an indication of the lack of female altruism in the matter of procreation.

9. *Consciously deliberated reasons for parenthood are often absent, especially among people who became parents several decades ago.* Approximately 15 percent of respondents in the two older groups stated that their first child happened accidentally. About 10 percent stated this of their second child. A little over 3 percent of respondents in the two older groups stated, with respect to their first child, "I thought that's what was expected in marriage."

Among write-in statements were variations of the following:

It never occurred to me not to have children.

I never thought of not having children.

All my friends were having babies.

10. *Younger women do not feel special needs to bear and rear offspring; older women do have such feelings to a moderate degree.* Approximately one-fourth of all women respondents over age 31 agreed that "to a moderate degree" there is a basic female need to be pregnant. (At least 18 percent of women over age 45 felt this to be so "to a high degree.") The response to this particular question from younger women was not significant. However, 90 percent of all female respondents stated there was "not at all" a need for women to be pregnant "every so often." Likewise, an equally emphatic negative response was made by such respondents to the question, "Was your desire to have a child prompted by wanting 'something to do'?" Thus, the negative responses to the questions concerning the need to be pregnant, and the need to be pregnant every so often might be negative indicators with respect to the presence of female egoism.

Although approximately 20 percent of women over age 31 "to a moderate degree" liked the attention pregnancy afforded them, and at least another one-third liked such attention "to a small degree," nearly 40 percent of those age 32 through 44 did not like such attention at all. Thus, in this instance, positive and negative indicators of female egoism seem to have cancelled each other.

11. *The capacity to procreate is not regarded as a sign of sexual maturity.* There was a high degree of consensus (86 percent) across all groups of respondents (including the men answering) that producing a child does not prove that a person is sexually mature. (Does this indicate absence of "machismo" among males in this country?)

12. *Procreation should be left to parental choice, not to chance or Divine Providence.* As indicated in Statement 6, over 85 percent of respondents disagreed strongly that people should leave procreation to chance or Divine Providence. Over 75 percent strongly agreed that married couples should have the right to decide whether or not to have children, and how many.

13. *Parents should have primary responsibility for care, support, protection, and entertainment of their children; there should be no bureaucratic interference with parental rights of procreation and nurture.* Most respondents indicated strongly that they wanted no governmental or UN interference with their parental right to procreate or refrain from procreating, and they were nearly unanimous in affirming that parents should have primary responsibility for care, support, protection, and entertainment of their children. Over 70 percent of respondents disagreed that raising children would be easier if directed by government standards or guidelines.

14. *Schools, churches, and other community institutions are regarded as supportive in the task of raising children.* Responses to this category came mostly from people over age 31. Over 70 percent of the two older groups found schools supportive, and over 80 percent of the same groups found church influence supportive. All respondents found other community organizations and combinations of them supportive. These included YMCA, YWCA, Girls' Clubs, Boys' Clubs, 4-H Clubs, public parks, and recreation services. Over 65 percent of respondents indicated that they did not feel schools were a threat to parental rights. Only 21 people (4 percent) strongly agreed that public schools do constitute such a threat.

15. *Overpopulation is a deterrent to procreation only after the birth of a first child.* Only 6 percent of respondents stated they were deterred from having their first child because of overpopulation; however, at least 15 percent gave overpopulation as a reason for not having a second child, 27 percent for not having a third, and 23 percent for not having a fourth.

16. *Money difficulties involving costs of raising children are not an appreciable cause of family disagreements, yet the high cost of raising children is an important deterrent to procreation.* Over 23 percent of all respondents gave high cost of raising a child as a prime reason for not having a first child; over 25 percent were deterred for this reason from having a second, 26 percent from having a third, and 23 percent from having a fourth. Yet, disagreements in the household were attributed by only 25 respondents to money difficulties involving costs of raising children. (Of these 25 respondents, 14 were over 45 years of age.)

17. *The traditional reason of being supported in old age by children is no longer cause for procreation.* Whether or not the availability of social security, Medicare, and so on, entered into consideration of respondents, over 95 percent of them answered "No" to the question, "Do you depend on their [your children] taking care of you when you are old?"

18. *Carrying on the family name or parental ideas or values are now not very important reasons for having children.* For respondents over age 25, parental expectations were high that their children would remain close to them in their old age; however, they did not purposely procreate in order to make this happen. The 4 respondents age 25 and younger were diveded evenly as to positive and negative expectations of having their children remain near them in their old age.

At least one-half of all respondents deemed not very important having children to carry on the family name or parental ideas and values

19. *Older people are more inclined to want to live near kinfolk than are younger people.* At least 15 percent of all respondents were strongly opposed to living close to kinfolk. Over 25 percent were opposed but with reservations. Of the 35 percent who approved, but with reservations, two-thirds were over age 31. Of the 12 percent who strongly approved living near kin, most were also over age 31.

20. *The nuclear family is still regarded as a good environment in which to raise children.* More than two-thirds of all respondents strongly disagreed with the statement that the nuclear family is no longer a fit environment in which to raise children, and an additional 18 percent disagreed with reservations. Only 18 people altogether agreed with the negative statement about the nuclear family. Thus, it would seem that there was near unanimity in favor of the nuclear family as a place of nurture for children.

21. *Older people are much less inclined than are younger ones to countenance the idea of an extended family that would include strangers.* There were only 31 people (6 percent) altogether who strongly agreed with the statement, "Some kind of contemporary extended family should be devised that would include non-blood related people, but would not

be exclusive [as are some contemporary 'communes'], but would countenance including strangers who happened to be neighbors in the vicinity." Of these respondents who strongly agreed, one-third were age 25 or under. An additional one-fourth of respondents agreed with the statement with reservations. Of the one-fourth who strongly disagreed, 68 percent were over age 31. There was another 17 percent who also disagreed, but with reservations. Of the one-fourth who strongly disagreed, 68 percent were over age 31. There was another 17 percent who also disageed, but with reservations. With respect to the survey sample, there was no significant indication that nonkin familism would be favored.

22. *Intentional family units without patriarchs are thought to be possible today.* Almost as many respondents strongly disagreed as strongly agreed that intentional family units without patriarchs are now possible; however, over one-fourth of all respondents agreed with reservations that this might be possible. Of the 15 percent strongly agreeing, 63 percent were under age 32, and 37 percent were age 32 or over.

23. *Personal and immediate family goals carry more weight than broader social aims; more emphasis is placed on community and neighborhood goals than on those of nation or world.* As was noted in Statement 7, prime goals of from 80 to 90 percent of all respondents were making a happy life for themselves and having interesting work to do. Having a happy family life was "highly important" or "most important" to 90 percent of all respondents. These and other responses shown in Tables 23–27 substantiate the primacy of personal and immediate family goals.

As shown by Table 27, higher percentages of all groups felt it "highly important" or "most important" to lend a hand to people in need in their neighborhoods or communities than to do so in the nation or the world. Also, about one-third of respondents thought it "highly important" or "most important" to help make their neighborhood a decent friendly place. Working with other people to bring brotherhood to the world was "highly important" or "most important" to about 28 percent of respondents. Thus, more emphasis was placed on community and neighborhood goals than on those of the nation or world.

24. *What children think their parents think of them is considered as important to children's self-images as what children think their peers think of them.* Respondents concluded, by strong agreement or agreement with some reservations, that these two factors are more or less equally important and are not mutually exclusive. This overlapping response might indicate a need to try to reconcile parental hopes with realities involved in "adolescent power" — an attempt to cope with strong

peer influence among teenagers today.

25. *There is no significant lack of parental attentiveness to children.* Data were obtained chiefly from respondents over age 25. From 70 to 80 percent of all respondents, including males, spent more than one hour a day playing or conversing with their children. Most respondents with children under age 15 regularly ate dinner with them, and children under 15 in families with parents over age 31 regularly had specific chores to do.

Although 31 percent of parents age 31 through 44 and 23 percent of parents over age 45 used television as a "babysitter" more than two hours per day, about one-fourth of parents over age 45 used grandparents for 23 percent of their babysitting, and generally across all parental age groups, one-third of respondents used combinations of grandparents, other relatives, and professional babysitters. People age 31 through 44 used television less than an hour a day, as did 40 percent of parents over age 45.

General Inferences from the Research

Since the exhaustive questionnaire was carefully completed by 45 percent of the people surveyed and was further annotated by many of the respondents, it may be inferred that the sample represents an identifiable microcosm that reflects, to some degree, attitudes and opinions of the general populace of the country with respect to the meaning of children in the contemporary United States.

The findings indicate that although Americans collectively countenance and also take part in social changes that adversely affect the family, as individuals they still cling to attitudes and opinions that place high value on children and on the nuclear family. Purported aspirations and goals still include hope of raising happy, healthy children for good citizenship. People having children would have no fewer if given a chance to do it over again. Yet, while individually valuing children and family, Americans as a group widely approve of and use contraceptives, vasectomy, and abortion. Futhermore, acting in society, they endorse easy dissolution of marriage, extralegal cohabitation, and pleasure-bonded marriage that excludes children, thus further demonstrating that their attitudes and opinions regarding family and children often do not match their public actions. More research would be required to discover substantive reasons for this evident discrepancy between what individuals are, and often believe, and how they act in society.

Since customs of long standing change slowly, it may be conjectured that the gap between individual attitudes and public actions may be only a manifestation of "cultural lag," and that current practices that may be detrimental to the integrity of the American family will gradually prevail, heralding even more diverse and unstable living patterns for the future. However, it also may be speculated that the discrepancy noted may be only apparent, not real, and that the enduring regard for children and parenthood may be indicative of a trend toward greater stability and homogeneity for the American family.

It can hardly be doubted, however, that human yearnings are being thwarted today by influences that seem to be beyond the individual's control. The general societal trends noted in Chapter 3 constantly and deeply affect the day-to-day life of everyone in the country. How Americans act, therefore, with respect to children and family, may be shaped more by societal impingements than by what individuals personally may want or try to do. In any event, since people in the United States, in spite of such buffetings, continue to have high regard for children and parenthood, the future for the American family may not be as bleak as is often supposed. Perhaps new, transitional forms of family life are emerging that now may seem to be soft underpinning for building a stable societal future, but which, nonetheless, have as hard core a strong affirmation of basic human values. Although contemporary adaptations of these values, as they relate to children and the family, may not always coincide with traditional notions, they do seem to reaffirm the existence of at least two perennial truths that are conducive to family building: *People want children and value them. Parental love is enduring.* Hence, it would seem that the strength and persistence of elements so basic to family structure and values will likely assure the survival of the familial community in the United States, despite detrimental forces to the contrary.

Bibliography

Books

Achebe, Chinua. *Things Fall Apart*. New York: Fawcett Publications, 1959, 1974.

Aries, Philippe. *Centuries of Childhood: A Social History of Family Life*. New York: Alfred A. Knopf, 1962.

Bellah, Robert N. *Beyond Belief*. New York: Harper & Row, 1970.

Benson, Mary S. *Women in Eighteenth Century America*. New York: Columbia University Press, 1935.

Berger, Peter L. *The Sacred Canopy: Elements of a Sociological Theory of Religion*. New York: Doubleday & Co., 1967.

Bernard, Jessie. *The Future of Marriage*. New York: Bantam World Publications Co., 1973.

Bossard, J. and E. Boll. *Ritual in Family Living*. Philadelphia: University of Pennsylvania Press, 1950.

Bowen, Elizabeth. *The Death of the Heart*. New York: Vantage Press, 1955.

Callahan, Sidney Cornelia. *Parenting: Principles and Politics of Parenthood*. New York: Doubleday & Co., 1973.

Capps, Walter H. *Time Invades the Cathedral*. Philadelphia: Fortress Press, 1972

Cott, Nancy F., ed. *Root of Bitterness*. New York: E. P. Dutton & Co., 1972.

Cox, Harvey. *The Secular City*. Rev. ed. New York: Macmillan, 1971.

_____. *The Seduction of the Spirit*. New York: Simon & Schuster, 1973.

Davis, Glenn. *Childhood and History in America*. New York: Psychohistory Press, 1976.

Dector, Midge. *The New Chastity*. New York: Berkley Medallion Pub. Corp., 1972.

de Rham, Edith. *The Love Fraud*. New York: Clarkson N. Potter, 1965.

Dewey, John. *School and Society*. Rev. ed. Chicago: University of Chicago Press, 1915.

Dickens, Charles. *American Notes*. New York: E. F. Collier, 1850 (?).

Durkheim, Emile. *Elementary Forms of Religious Life*. London: Allen & Unwin, 1954.

Encyclopaedia Britannica. 15th ed. 1974. Macropaedia, vols. 6, 8, 13.

Flexner, Eleanor. *Century of Struggle*. New York: Atheneum, 1974.

Freud, Sigmund. "Civilization and Its Discontents." *Encyclopaedia Britannica, Great Books of the Western World.* vol. 54. 1952, pp. 767–802.

Fuchs, Lawrence, H. *Family Matters.* New York: Warner Paperback Library, 1974.

Gabriel, Ralph Henry. *The Course of American Democratic Thought.* New York: Ronald Press, 1956.

Gadamer, H. C. *Warheit und Methode.* Tübingen: Siebeck & Mohr, 1972. vol. 11.

Galbraith, John Kenneth. "Consumption and the Concept of the Household." *Economics and the Public Purpose.* Boston: Houghton Mifflin, 1973, pp. 31–40.

Gaylin, Willard, *Caring.* New York: Alfred A. Knopf, 1976.

Gilder, George. *Naked Nomads: Unmarried Men in America.* New York: N.Y. Times Book Co., 1974.

Goldberg, Steven. *The Inevitability of Patriarchy.* New York: William Morrow & Co., 1973.

Great Books of the Western World, Chicago: Encyclopaedia Britannica, vol. 35.

Greven, Philip J. Jr., *Four Generations: Population, Land, and Family in Colonial Andover, Mass.* Ithaca, N.Y.: Cornell University Press, 1970.

Hawthorne, Nathaniel. *The Scarlet Letter.* Boston: Houghton Mifflin, 1883.

Heidegger, Martin. *Discourse on Thinking.* New York: Harper & Row, 1959.

Hess, Robert D. and G. Handel. *Family Worlds.* Chicago: University of Chicago Press, 1959

Hollinshead, August B. *Elmtown's Youth and Elmtown Revisited.* New York: John Wiley & Sons, 1949, 1975.

Hunt, Morton M. *The Natural History of Love.* New York: Alfred A. Knopf, 1959.

Hutchins, Robert M. *The Learning Society.* New York: Praeger Publishers, 1968.

Illich, Ivan D. *Medical Nemesis: The Expropriation of Health.* London: Calder & Boyars, Ltd., 1975.

————. *Deschooling Society.* New York: Harper & Row, 1971.

Larus, John Rouse. *Woman: In All Ages and In All Countries.* Women in America series, vol. 10. Philadelphia: George Barrie & Sons, 1908.

Laslett, Peter. *The World We Have Lost: England Before the Industrial Age.* New York: Charles Scribner's Sons, 1965, 1971.

Lear, Martha Weinman. *The Child Worshippers.* New York: Crown Publishers, 1963.

Le Masters, E. E. *Parents in Modern America.* Homewood, Ill.: Dorsey Press, 1970.

Lerner, Gerda. *The Grimke Sisters.* New York: Schocken Books, 1971.

Liebow, Elliot, "Husbands and Wives." *Tally's Corner.* New York: Little, Brown and Co., 1966.

Linder, Staffan. B. *The Harried Leisure Class.* New York: Columbia University Press, 1970.

Lockridge, Kenneth A. *A New England Town–The First Hundred Years.* New York: W. W. Norton & Co., 1970

Lyford, Joseph P. *The Airtight Cage.* New York: Harper & Row, 1966.

MacIntyre, Alasdair. *Secularization and Moral Change.* London: Oxford University Press, 1967.

Masters, William H. and Virginia E. Johnson. *The Pleasure Bond.* Boston: Little, Brown and Co., 1974.

Mead, Margaret. *Male and Female.* New York: William Morrow & Co., 1968.

Michaelsen, Robert. *Piety in the Public School.* New York: Macmillan, 1970.

Miller, S. M. *Max Weber.* New York: Thomas Y. Crowell Co., 1963.

Mitchell, Juliet. *Psychoanalysis and Feminism: Freud, Reich, Laing and Women.* New York: Pantheon Books, 1974.

Morgan, Edmund S. *The Puritan Family.* New York: Harper Torchbooks, 1966.

Murdock, George Peter. *Social Structure.* New York: Macmillan, 1960.

Nisbet, Robert A. *The Sociological Tradition.* New York: Basic Books, 1966.

Ogburn, William F. and M. F. Nimkoff. "The Family," "Religious Institutions," and "Interrelationship of Institutions." *Sociology.* Boston: Houghton Mifflin, 1950.

Olsen, Tillie. *Tell Me A Riddle.* New York: Dell Publishing Co., 1961.

_____ . *Yonnondio: From the Thirties.* New York: Dell Publishing Co., 1975.

O'Neill, Nena & George. *Open Marriage.* New York: Avon Books, 1972.

Potter, J. "Growth of Population in America, 1700–1860." *Population in History — Essays in History.* Edited by Glass and Eversley. Chicago: University of Chicago Press, 1965.

Queen, Stuart A. and Robert W. Habenstein. *The Family in Various Cultures.* 3rd. ed. Philadelphia: Lippincott, 1967.

Rapoport, Rhona and Robert N. Rapoport with Streliz, Ziona. *Leisure and the Family Life Cycle.* London & Boston: Routledge & Kegan Paul, 1975.

Robinson, J. and J. Cobb. *The New Hermeneutic.* New York: Harper & Row, 1964.

Rolvaag, O. E. *Giants in the Earth.* New York: Harper & Row Perennial Classics, 1927.

Rosaldo, Michelle Zimbalist. *Woman, Culture, and Society.* Edited by Louise Lamphere. Stanford, Calif.: Stanford University Press, 1974.

Rousseau, Jean Jacques. *Emile: Emilius, or a Treatise of Education, Translated from the French of J. J. Rousseau.* Edinburgh, 1773. Printed for W. Coke, Bookseller in Leith, 1762.

Rowbotham, Sheila. *Woman's Consciousness, Man's World.* Baltimore, Md.: Penguin Books, 1973.

Sedgwick, Catherine. "A Glimpse at Family Government." *Home.* Boston: James Munroe & Co., 1835.

Sheehy, Gail. *Passages: Predictable Crises of Adult Life.* New York: E. P. Dutton & Co., 1976.

Silverman, Anna and Arnold. *The Case Against Having Children.* New York: David McKay Co., Inc., 1971.

Skolnick, Arlene. *The Intimate Environment.* Boston: Little, Brown and Co., 1973.

Skolnick, Arlene S. and Jerome K. *Family in Transition.* Boston: Little, Brown and Co., 1971.

Smith, James R. and Lynn G. *Beyond Monogamy.* Baltimore, Md.: Johns Hopkins University Press, 1974.

Stephens, William N. *The Family in Cross-Cultural Perspective.* New York: Holt, Rinehart and Winston, 1963.

Stowe, Harriet Beecher. *Uncle Tom's Cabin.* New York: Signet–New American Library, 1966.

Thompson, William Irwin. *Passages About Earth: An Exploration of the New Planetary Culture.* New York: Harper & Row, 1974.

Tuchman, Barbara. *The Proud Tower.* New York: Macmillian, 1966.

Udry, J. Richard. *The Social Context of Marriage.* 2nd ed. Philadelphia: Lippincott, 1971.

Weber, Max. *Basic Concepts in Sociology.* Translated by H. P. Secher. New York: Citadel Press, 1966.

Welter, Barbara, ed. *The Woman Question In America History.* Hinsdale, Ill.: Dryden Press, 1973.

Wishy, Bernard. *The Child and the Republic.* Philadelphia: University of Pennsylvania Press, 1972.

Zimmerman, Carle C. *Family and Civilization.* New York: Harper & Brothers, 1947.

Manuscripts and Collections

Readings on *Hermeneutics* in writings of the following authors: Hans-Georg Gadamer, Jürgen Habermas, W. J. McCutcheon, David E. Linge, Wilhelm Dilthey, Carl E. Braaten, James M. Robinson, Ernst Fuchs, Gerhard Ebeling, and Paul Ricoeur.

19th Century New Englanders. Selections from four diaries and four autobiographies including young people and adults: David Clapp, Benjamin Champney, Hiram Munger, Elizabeth Fuller, Samuel Goodright, Moses Porter, Horace Greeley, Samantha Barrett. (From Old Sturbridge Museum Collections, Old Sturbridge Village, Mass.)

Periodicals

Ballad, Richard. "The Testimony of Ivan Illich." *Human Behavior,* Feb., 1977.

Boeth, Richard. *Newsweek*, Mar. 12, 1973, p. 56.

Bolton, Charles D. "Mate Selection as the Development of a Relationship." *Marriage and Family Living,* August, 1961.

Brobeck, Stephen. "Images of the Family: Portrait Paintings as Indices of American Family Culture, Structure and Behavior, 1730–1860." *The Journal of Psychohistory,* 5, no. 1, Summer, 1977, pp. 81–106.

Chafe, William H. "Feminism in the 1970's." *Dissent,* Fall, 1974.

Danziger, Carl and Matthew Greenwald. "A Look at Unmarried Couples." *Agape,* August, 1974.

Delooz, Pierre. "The Western Family: A Prospective Evaluation." *Cross Currents,* Winter, 1974.

Demaitre, Luke. "The Idea of Childhood and Child Care in Medical Writings of the Middle Ages." *The Journal of Psychohistory,* 4, no. 4, Spring, 1977, pp. 461–490.

Demos, John. "The American Family in Past Time." *The American Scholar,* Summer, 1974.

Ebel, Henry. "The Evolution of Childhood Reconsidered." *The Journal of Psychohistory,* 5, no. 1, Summer, 1977, pp. 67–80.

Elshtain, Jean Bethke. "Moral Woman and Immoral Man: A Consideration of the Public-Private Split and Its Political Ramification." *Politics and Society,* 1974, pp. 453–473.

Grossman, Edward, "The Family in the Tube." *World Magazine,* Mar. 13, 1973, p. 54.

Hareven, Tamara K. "The Historical Study of the Family Cycle." 13th International Seminar of the Committee of Family Research of the International Sociological Assn., Paris, Sept., 1973; as reported in *Family in Historical Perspective,* Spring, 1974.

Hendin, Herbert. "The New Anomie." *Change* (Nov. 1975) in *The Age of Sensation.* New York: W. W. Norton Co., 1975.

History of Childhood Quarterly: *Journal of Psychohistory,* 2, no. 4, Spring, 1975; 3, no. 1, Summer, 1975; 3, no. 2, Fall, 1975.

Hunt, Morton. "Sexual Behavior in the 1970's." *Playboy*, Oct., 1973.

Journal of Psychohistory, 3, no. 1, Summer, 1975; 4, no. 1, Summer, 1976; 3, no. 3, Winter, 1976; 4, no. 4, Spring, 1977; and 5, no. 1, Summer, 1977.

Kass, Leon R. "The Family: A Final Solution?" *The Public Interest,* no. 26, Winter, 1972.

Lasch, Christopher. "The Emotions of Family Life." *N. Y. Review,* November 27, 1975.

_____ . "The Family and History." *N. Y. Review,* Nov. 13, 1975.

Lerner, Max. Column in *Santa Barbara News Press,* Dec. 14, 1977, p. F–12.

O'Connor, John. *New York Times,* Jan. 23, 1973, p. 79.

Minuchin, Dr. Salvador. "Vast Majority of Americans Still Believe in the Family." *U.S. News & World Report,* Jan. 13, 1975.

Modell, John. "Economic Dimensions of Family History." 13th International Seminar of the Committee of Family Research of the International Sociological Assn., Paris, Sept., 1973; as reported in *Family in Historical Perspective,* Spring, 1974.

Newsweek, Mar. 12, 1973, pp. 55, 57.

Podhoretz, Norman. "The Return of Success." *Newsweek,* August 29, 1977, p. 11.

Proctor, Pam. "Dr. Karl Menninger Pleads: Stop Beating Your Kids." *Parade,* Oct. 9, 1977, pp. 304–305.

Reeves, Thomas C. "Religion and Reformers." *The Living Church.* June 5, 1977.

Roper, Survey. "Sex . . . Marriage . . . Divorce—What Women Think Today."
   U.S. News & World Report, October 21, 1974.
Rothman, David J. "A Note On the Study of the Colonial Family." *William and Mary Quarterly,* 23, October, 1966, pp. 627–634.
Saveth, Edward N. "The Problem of American Family History." *American Quarterly,* Summer, 1969, pp. 311–329.
Schwartz, Tony. "Women and Men: No More Absolutes." *Change,* October, 1974.
Skolnick, Arlene. "What is the History of the Family the History of?" 13th International Seminar of the Committee of Family Research of the International Sociological Assn., Paris, Sept., 1973; as reported in *Family in Historical Perspective,* Spring, 1974.
"Throwaway Marriages: Threat to the American Family. *"U.S. News & World Report,* Jan. 13, 1975.
True, M. and J. Young. "Divorce and Remarriage." *Commonweal,* Nov. 22, 1974.
Yankelovich, Daniel and Ruth Clark. "College and Noncollege Youth Values." *Change,* Sept., 1974.

Public Documents

National Center for Health Statistics. *Vital Statisics Report,* vol. 24, no. 13, June 30, 1976.
National Center for Health Statistics. *Vital Statistics Report,* vol. 26, no. 2, May, 19, 1977; no. 5, Aug. 10, 1977.
National Center for Health Statistics. *Vital Statistics Report,* vol. 25, no. 10, Dec. 30, 1976.